" . . . all in our little company agreed, it was the finest view
any of us had beheld in the Rockies."

—Mary Schäffer, 1908

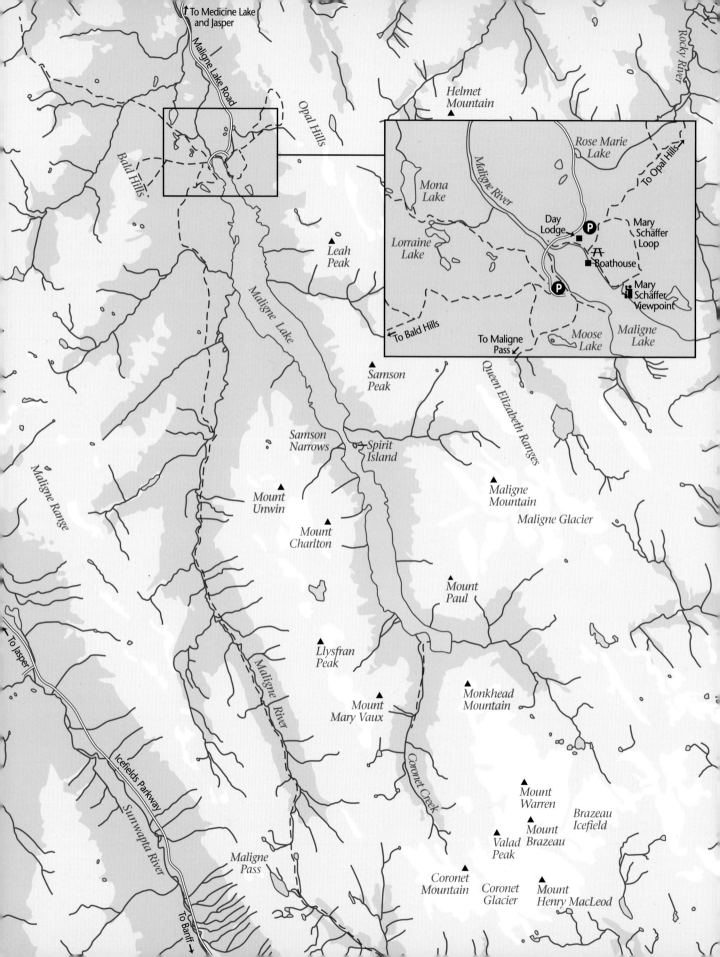

Contents

With its breathtaking mountain setting and an abundance of wildlife, Maligne Lake surely ranks among the great natural wonders of the world. Tour boats bound for Spirit Island glide across crystal-clear water, adventurous visitors set out in canoes and kayaks for secluded coves, and anglers cast for trophy-sized trout. Hikers head out on well-formed trails along the lake to panoramic viewpoints and into the surrounding emerald forest and cross fast-flowing streams to emerge at picturesque lakes. However you choose to experience the jewel of Jasper National Park, Maligne Lake serves up a veritable feast of memorable experiences.

Looking across Maligne Lake to the Bald Hills

Nature at its Finest

SURROUNDED BY SOARING PEAKS CAPPED BY A BLANKET OF SNOW WELL INTO SUMMER, AND DRAINED BY THE SWIFT-FLOWING MALIGNE RIVER, MALIGNE LAKE IS ONE OF THE MOST BEAUTIFUL PLACES IN THE CANADIAN ROCKIES.

Pronounced "Muh-leen," this famous, scenic lake lies in the heart of the Canadian Rockies. The Canadian Rockies are part of the Rocky Mountains, which extend northward from near Sante Fe, New Mexico, to the Liard River, which runs along the boundary between British Columbia and the Yukon. The spine of these mountains is the Continental Divide (also known as the Great Divide). Through Jasper National Park, this crest of mountains divides Pacific drainage from Arctic drainage. Along the western edge of Jasper National Park, the divide also forms a natural border between British Columbia and Alberta.

The Birth of the Canadian Rockies

The Rocky Mountains began rising 100 million years ago, which makes them middle-aged compared to the world's other major mountain ranges. But to fully appreciate the geology of the Rocky Mountains, you must look back many hundreds of millions of years to the Proterozoic Era. Approximately 740 million years ago, an ocean covered the area where the Canadian Rockies now stand. The ocean advanced and then receded many times over the next 600 million years. Each time the ocean flooded eastward, it deposited layers of silt and sand on its bed—layers that built up with each successive flood. Over time, the ever-increasing sediment load compressed the underlying layers, and this compression created the sedimentary rock found throughout the region today.

Some 375 million years ago, the stability of the ocean floor began wavering along what was then the west coast of North America (not far west of where the Canadian Rockies are now located). This instability culminated 210 million years ago in a plate collision. According to plate tectonics theory, the earth's crust is broken into several massive chunks (plates) that are always moving and occasionally collide. This is not an event that happens overnight; a plate may move only a few centimetres per year.

In the case of the Rocky Mountains, plates underlying the western Pacific Ocean were

AT A GLANCE

At 22.3 kilometres (13.8 miles) long, Maligne Lake is the largest body of water in Jasper National Park and the largest natural lake in the Canadian Rockies. Its maximum depth is 97 metres (318 feet) and its maximum width is two kilometres (1.2 miles). At the aptly named Samson Narrows, the lake is just 100 metres (330 feet) wide. Maligne Lake sits at an elevation of 1,675 metres (5,495 feet) above sea level, around 500 metres (1,640 feet) higher than the town of Jasper. During the summer, the water temperature along the shoreline rises above 10°C (50°F), but deep below the surface, the water temperature is just 4°C (39°F).

Queen Elizabeth Ranges

forced underneath the North American Plate. The land above this collision zone and eastward into Alberta was crumpled and thrust upward, which created the mountains of western Canada, including the Canadian Rockies. The layers of sedimentary rock that had been deposited on the seabed over the course of hundreds of millions of years were folded, twisted, and squeezed; great slabs of rock broke loose and were pushed up and over younger layers. By the beginning of the Paleogene Period, around 65 million years ago, the geological framework of the mountains was in place. Erosion continued to shape the landscape into the mountains we see today.

It is easy to identify the layers of siltstone, limestone, dolostone, shale, and quartzite in the mountains. Each of these sedimentary rocks has different properties and offers an insight into the natural history it represents. Siltstone is composed of compressed particles (smaller than sand particles). Shale is another fine-grained sedimentary rock. It is made mostly of hardened clay and other small mineral particles. Shale, which breaks easily along thin layers, can be many different colours, including black, red, brown, and green. The colour variations are due mainly to the presence, or lack thereof, of iron. Some of the limestone and dolostone layers are rich in chert, which is a micro-crystalline sedimentary rock that often contains small fossils. It is rich in silica and is usually black or grey in the Jasper area. Chert was prized by prehistoric people, who used it to make stone tools. It was also used to start fires, as it consistently produced sparks when chipped against metal.

Limestone, another sedimentary rock common in the Maligne Valley, is made up of the mineral calcite, which was mostly deposited as tiny crystals by microscopic marine organisms. The solubility of limestone makes it particularly prone to water erosion—in areas where limestone is found there are sure to be canyons and caves, such as in the lower reaches of the Maligne River.

MOUNTAIN HIGH

The highest peak in the Maligne Lake area is Mount Brazeau, which at 3,470 metres (11,386 feet) just misses being included on the list of the 10 highest mountains in the Canadian Rockies.

The highest point in the Canadian Rockies is the summit of Mount Robson, but this is not the highest peak in Canada; this honour is claimed by 5,959-metre (19,550-foot) Mount Logan in the Yukon. Mount Waddington in the Coast Ranges is also higher, at 4,016-metres (13,177 feet).

The 10 highest mountains in the Canadian Rockies are as follows

Mount Robson	Mount Robson Provincial Park	3,954 m (12,972 ft)
Mount Columbia	Jasper National Park	3,747 m (12,293 ft)
North Twin Peak	Jasper National Park	3,684 m (12,087 ft)
Mount Clemenceau	Jasper National Park	3,658 m (12,001 ft)
Mount Alberta	Jasper National Park	3,619 m (11,873 ft)
Mount Assiniboine	Banff National Park	3,618 m (11,870 ft)
Mount Forbes	Banff National Park	3,612 m (11,850 ft)
South Twin Peak	Jasper National Park	3,566 m (11,700 ft)
Mount Temple	Banff National Park	3,543 m (11,624 ft)
Goodsir Towers	Yoho National Park	3,525 m (11,565 ft)

The Ice Ages

Around three million years ago, the world's climate cooled by a few degrees. Ice caps formed in the northern regions and slowly moved southward over North America and Eurasia. These advances, which were followed by retreats, occurred many times. During the greater advances, all of what is now Jasper National Park, including the Maligne Valley, was covered in ice.

Around 31,000 years ago, the most recent major glaciation began. A sheet of ice approximately 2,000 metres (6,560 feet) thick covered all but the highest peaks of the Canadian Rockies. Like many glaciers today, this massive sheet of ice began receding ever so slowly as the earth warmed and scoured the landscape, rounded off lower peaks, and carved valleys from their pre-glacial V-shapes into U-shapes. The rounded Bald Hills, easily identified to the west of Maligne Lake's northern end, are a classic example of glacial action.

The Athabasca River Valley, in which the town of Jasper lies, is typical of a U-shaped glacially carved valley. The Maligne Valley is a hanging valley that was carved by a tributary glacier. The main glacier covered the Athabasca River Valley and cut away its side, which resulted in the distinct elevation differences between the two valleys and a swift-flowing river that drops steeply into the Athabasca River Valley.

Maligne Lake is a result of glaciation both directly and indirectly. The deep southern part of the lake is a huge, glacially carved basin in the bedrock, and the natural dam at the northern end is made of rock debris from several large rockslides caused indirectly by glacial erosion. During the last Ice Age, as a massive glacier flowed down the Maligne Valley, layers of sedimentary rock on the east

*Boulders along Maligne Lake Road
are from an ancient rockslide*

side of the valley were undercut by the erosive power of the glacial ice. Less than 14,000 years ago, the instability of these layers led to a series of massive landslides—among the largest to ever occur in the Canadian Rockies. One of these, tumbling from the Queen Elizabeth Ranges, spread an estimated half a billion cubic metres (17.6 billion cubic feet) of rock 3.7 kilometres (2.3 miles) across the Maligne Valley. This slide, along with another from the rust-coloured Opal Hills, formed a natural dam that made Maligne Lake longer and deeper. House-sized boulders from this and other ancient slides can be seen beside Maligne Lake Road and on the lake's western shore.

Opal Hills

WHAT IS A MORAINE?

As glaciers move, they carry rock debris. When a glacier begins receding, this debris is deposited as a mound or ridge known as a moraine.

There are many different types of moraines, and two are common in the Canadian Rockies. Lateral moraines are ridges that run parallel to the path of the glacier. Terminal (or "end") moraines are composed of debris left at the toe of the glacier as it recedes. If glacial retreat stops, more rock will accumulate and the terminal moraine eventually left behind will be larger.

Lateral moraine

Maligne Lake Glaciers

A number of glaciers cling to mountain slopes high above Maligne Lake. Remnants of the sheet of ice that once covered the valley, these glaciers are mostly scattered around the southern half of the lake. Within view of the day lodge, the glacier between Mounts Charlton and Unwin displays many of the classic geological features of a typical glacier. At the apex is a dome glacier, and hanging glaciers lie between the two peaks. The receding ice piles rocks into high lateral moraines. Across the lake is the Maligne Glacier, which has carved a massive cirque out of the upper slopes of Maligne Mountain.

Beyond the south end of Maligne Lake is the Brazeau Icefield. Mount Brazeau, 3,470 metres (11,386 feet) high, sits at its head. From the lake, the icefield and mountain are mostly blocked from view by Monkhead Mountain, which rises dramatically from the lakeshore. Feeding both Maligne Lake and the Brazeau River, the Brazeau Icefield is the largest in the Front Ranges of the Canadian Rockies. Southwest of the Brazeau Icefield, the slopes below the Coronet Glacier exhibit extensive moraines. Although a rough trail leads up Coronet Creek from the lakeshore, this is a remote area visited only by experienced backcountry enthusiasts.

The meltwater from these glaciers drains into Maligne Lake, deposits glacial sediment, and forms alluvial fans. Over thousands of years, the amount of sediment settling into the lake has changed the lakeshore, and the effects are most dramatic at Samson Narrows, the narrowest part of the lake, which is about 100 metres (330 feet) wide. If the glaciers on either

A moose visits Maligne Lake at dawn.

side of the narrows keep receding, sand and gravel will continue to build up. Eventually, Maligne Lake could be totally divided into two bodies of water.

One of the most obvious signs that a lake is glacially fed is the stunning turquoise colour of the water, which is due to high concentrations of glacial silt. This sediment is as fine as flour (hence the term "rock flour"). The silt, which has been ground from bedrock by moving ice, is so fine that it does not sink immediately to the bottom of the lake; instead, it is temporarily suspended in the water. Varying concentrations of silt result in variations in colour between lakes and even within one lake, as the rate of changing air temperatures increases and decreases glacial melt through the year.

Maligne Lake is such a large body of water that the colour changes dramatically from one end to the other. South of Samson Narrows, below two receding glaciers, the water has a high concentration of silt and is a brilliant turquoise colour throughout summer, while at the north end, near the tour boat complex, the water is clearer.

The Seasons

Jasper National Park has four distinct seasons, including short, relatively hot summers and long, cold winters. While spring arrives in the lower valleys by late April, Maligne Lake remains frozen, and its surrounding shore, including the Bald Hills and the Opal Hills, remains covered in snow until well into May. Usually, Maligne Lake is not totally thawed until late May or the first week of June. Generally, spring is a rainy time of year, and precipitation falls as snow at higher elevations.

The summer solstice, June 21, is officially the first day of summer. On this day, the longest of the year, Maligne Lake enjoys almost 17 hours of sunlight. July is the warmest month in the park, with an average daytime temperature above 23°C (73°F). On the hottest summer days, the temperature rises above 30°C (86°F) along lower-elevation valleys. These temperatures are more bearable in the mountains than in coastal regions due to the dryness of the air. Throughout the summer, outdoor enthusiasts take full advantage of the long, warm days at Maligne Lake and spend as much time as possible hiking, canoeing, kayaking, fishing, and camping.

With its bracing, fresh air, autumn (usually known as "fall" in North America) is a transitional season. Due to the lack of crowds at this time of year, September, the first month of autumn, is a great time to visit Jasper National Park and is the last chance to experience Maligne Lake by boat. Although the cruises and rentals offered by Maligne Tours end in early October, the lake is still accessible and can be enjoyed well into autumn. With less traffic on Maligne Lake Road, this is a good time to see wildlife such as elk, moose, deer, bighorn sheep, and bears feeding before the valley is blanketed with snow.

By late September, the mountain air has a distinct chill and morning frost is common. The highest temperature variations of the year occur in October; the temperature has reached 30°C (86°F) in the Athabasca River Valley, but can also dip as low as -20°C (-4°F). September snowfalls are not uncommon at higher elevations, and by late November, winter has set in throughout the Maligne Valley. The surrounding mountains draw the moisture out of the air and down into the valley. Maligne Lake is usually frozen by late November.

Frost on the dock at Maligne Lake is a sign of fall

The winter solstice, December 21, marks the shortest day of the year. At lower elevations, it is dark by 4:00 p.m., and at Maligne Lake, the sun begins to disappear behind the mountains by 3 p.m. January is the park's coldest month. The average daily low is -17.8°C (1.4°F), although it will often get as cold as -30°C (-22°F) for a few days. Very rarely, temperatures may drop below -40°C (-40°F). Severe cold weather is often accompanied by sunshine; the cold is a dry cold, unlike the damp cold experienced in coastal regions.

Snow blankets the Maligne Valley throughout winter. Maligne Lake Road remains open and is cleared all the way to Maligne Lake, where cross-country skiers set out for day trips across the lake and into the Bald Hills.

HIGHER IS COOLER

One of the biggest factors influencing temperature within Jasper National Park is elevation. As you gain elevation, the temperature decreases. Generally there is a loss of 1.7°C (4°F) for every 300 metres (1,000 feet) of elevation gained. Maligne Lake is approximately 500 metres (1,640 feet) higher than the town of Jasper, so temperatures at the lake are usually significantly cooler than in town.

Moose at Moose Lake

Wildflowers and Wildlife

ADDING TO THE BEAUTY OF MALIGNE LAKE AND ITS SURROUNDING MOUNTAINS ARE THE SUBALPINE FORESTS, COLOURFUL WILDFLOWERS, AND AN ABUNDANCE OF WILDLIFE.

Trees and Flowers

Botanists divide the Canadian Rockies into three distinct vegetation zones: montane, subalpine, and alpine. The boundaries of these zones are determined by several factors, the most important being altitude. Latitude and exposure are also factors. Typically, within 1,500 metres (4,920 feet) of elevation change, you will pass through all three zones.

In the Canadian Rockies, the montane zone occurs along the floors of lower valleys, such as the area of the Athabasca River Valley where the road to Maligne Lake begins. The forests in this zone are comprised of aspen, balsam poplar, white spruce, and lodgepole pine, the most common tree in the zone. The lodgepole pine is named for its straight trunk, which the Aboriginal people valued for building tepees. Maligne Lake Road passes through typical montane environment between Highway 16 and the turn-off to Maligne Canyon's Sixth Bridge.

The subalpine zone, in which Maligne Lake lies, tends to have a lower average temperature and a higher average level of precipitation than the montane. Maligne Lake sits at an elevation of 1,675 metres (5,495 feet), well within the subalpine zone, which generally occurs between 1,500 and 2,200 metres (4,920 and 7,220 feet) above sea level. The upper limit of the subalpine zone is identified as the treeline, which can be clearly seen from the day lodge when looking west to the Bald Hills. Most of the trees around the north end of the lake are conifers, and lodgepole pine is the dominant species. Subalpine fir and white spruce are

WILDLIFE SAFETY

Viewing wildlife is one of the highlights of visiting Jasper National Park, but wild animals are unpredictable. In order to minimize the amount of disturbance to animals and to view them safely, keep the following rules in mind:
- Drive carefully. The most common cause of premature death for larger mammals is being hit by cars.
- Use roadside pullouts when viewing wildlife from a vehicle.
- Keep a safe distance. Use binoculars or telephoto lenses.
- Do not feed the animals. Although they may seem tame, feeding them endangers yourself and the animal.
- Store food safely. When picnicking or camping, keep food in your vehicle or out of reach of animals.

A "bear jam" along Maligne Lake Road

Canada geese, with Mounts Charlton and Unwin rising from the far shore of Maligne Lake

Crystal-clear streams flow through the subalpine forest before draining into Maligne Lake

also present, while at the remote south end of the lake, where visitors rarely tread, there are stands of Engelmann spruce thought to be up to 600 years old. On the cool, shaded subalpine forest floor, mosses, lichens, and mushrooms thrive.

The Bald Hills are an easily accessible example of the alpine zone, which extends from the treeline to the mountain summits. The Bald Hills can be reached on foot from Maligne Lake in under two hours. The upper limit of tree growth in the Canadian Rockies varies between 1,800 and 2,400 metres (5,900 and 7,900 feet) above sea level. Tree growth progressively drops to the north up to the treeless tundra of the Arctic. Vegetation at these high altitudes occurs only where soil has been deposited. Large areas of alpine meadows burst with colour for a short period each summer, as a variety of heathers and other intensely coloured wildflowers bloom briefly.

WILDFLOWERS

Potentilla (also known as snow cinquefoil) is a beautiful yellow flower that grows in both subalpine and alpine areas of the Maligne Valley; look for these flowers along the lakeshore beyond the boathouse from late June until late August. Flowering in the same season is Indian paintbrush, a red or orange flower that grows prolifically along Maligne Lake Road. Bunches of white-flowered Labrador tea are common along streams in subalpine forests but also grow in the lower areas of the alpine zone.

One of the Maligne Valley's most beautiful flowers is the Calypso orchid (also known as Venus's slipper), a light pink or purple flower found in shaded montane and subalpine forests from May through June.

The best time for viewing wildflowers in the alpine zone is late July and early August. One of the first to bud is the red-stemmed saxifrage. Other alpine flowers you may see above the treeline around Maligne Lake include common harebells, arnica, western springbeauty, forget-me-nots, mountain heather, and moss campion.

BERRIES

As berries begin ripening in late summer, they attract bears, which gorge on them at an amazing rate. Common species in the Maligne Valley include bearberries, bunchberries, and dwarf raspberries.

Top: flowering bunchberry
Middle: arnica
Lower: Labrador tea

Opposite: Mosses thrive in the cool, damp, subalpine forests around Maligne Lake

Wildlife

An important wildlife corridor, the Maligne Valley offers visitors plenty of opportunities to observe and photograph a wide variety of animals and birds in their natural habitat. When driving on Maligne Lake Road, it is not uncommon to see deer, elk, bighorn sheep, and bears. Moose are relatively common around the lake itself, while at higher elevations, marmots and pikas inhabit rocky areas. Although Maligne Lake was originally known by the Stoney of the Kootenay Plains as "Chaba Imne" (Beaver Lake), the industrious aquatic mammals the lake is named for are not likely to be seen (they are more common in the Athabasca River Valley).

The wildlife in the valley changes according to the time of year and even the time of day. Spring is an especially good time to spot bears feeding by the roadside, while elk tend to congregate at the lower (north) end of the valley each fall. In the hours immediately after dawn and before dusk, the chances of spotting wildlife are far greater than during the middle of the day. In the winter, when the Maligne Valley is covered in snow, wolves can occasionally be seen. At this time of year, bears are hibernating and other larger mammals, such as elk and deer, move to lower elevations, where there is less snow cover.

DEER

Five species of deer inhabit Jasper National Park: white-tailed and mule deer, elk, moose, and, caribou. All five species are present in the Maligne Valley. The white-tailed deer's tail is dark on top, but when the animal runs, it holds its tail erect, which reveals an all-white underside. These deer frequent thickets along rivers and lakes as well as montane forests. The mule deer, known for its large ears, is commonly seen around the edge of the town or grazing in open forests and meadows. During the summer, this species is most often seen at the north end of Maligne Lake Road in the vicinity of Maligne Canyon.

Elk are common at lower elevations

ELK

A member of the deer family, the elk (also known as wapiti) is the most widespread and common larger mammal living in the Canadian Rockies. (The town of Jasper is in the home range of about 500 elk, which can be seen year-round around town boundaries and northeast along Highway 16). Elk are often seen along the northern end of Maligne Lake Road, between Maligne Canyon and Highway 16. The best opportunities for viewing them are in fall and winter, when they congregate at lower elevations throughout the park. Snow cover is not as deep at these elevations, which makes feeding and movement easier. Elk have tan-coloured bodies, dark-brown necks and legs, and white rumps. This second-largest member of the deer family weighs 250–450 kilograms (550–1,000 pounds) and stand 1.5 metres (five feet) at the shoulder. Each spring, stags grow an impressive set of antlers that are covered in what is known as velvet. The velvet contains nutrients that stimulate antler growth. By fall, the antlers have reached their full size and the velvet is shed. Rutting season takes place in the fall; at this time of year, listen for the shrill bugles of the stags as they serenade the females.

MOOSE

The largest member of the deer family is the moose, an awkward-looking mammal that appears to have been designed by a cartoonist. Numbering around 100 in Jasper National Park, they are active in the Maligne Valley year-round. Moose are solitary animals that prefer marshy areas and weedy lakes, such as Moose Lake. The moose has the largest antlers of any animal in the world, stands up to 1.8 metres (six feet) at the shoulder, and weighs up to 500 kilograms (1,100 pounds). Its body is dark brown, and it has a prominent nose, long spindly legs, small eyes, big ears, and an odd flap of skin called a bell dangling beneath its chin. Each spring, the bull begins to grow palm-shaped antlers that by August will be fully grown.

Moose

MOUNTAIN GOATS

The remarkable rock-climbing ability of these nimble-footed creatures allows them to live on rocky ledges or near-vertical slopes, safe from predators. Scan the distant mountain slopes with binoculars as you cruise down Maligne Lake and you may spot them. They also congregate at natural salt licks, such as the one south of Athabasca Falls beside the Icefields Parkway. The goat stands one metre (3.3 feet) at the shoulder and weighs 65–130 kilograms (140–290 pounds). Both sexes possess a peculiar beard, or rather, "goatee."

Mountain goat

Bighorn sheep are easily recognized by their massive curled horns

BIGHORN SHEEP

Easily recognizable by the male's impressive horns, bighorn sheep are among the most distinctive mammals living in the Canadian Rockies. A reliable place to see them in the summer is where Maligne Lake Road passes alongside Medicine Lake. (The sheep are particularly tolerant of humans and will often approach parked vehicles or those stopped on the road; although they are not especially dangerous, as with all mammals, you should not approach or feed them). The colour of their coat varies with the season; in summer, it's a brownish grey, and the belly and rump are cream-coloured. Its colour lightens in the winter. Both sexes possess horns (rather than antlers, like members of the deer family), which are not shed each year. The spiraled horns of older rams grow to astounding sizes: they can measure up to one metre (3.3 feet) and weigh as much as 15 kilograms (33 pounds).

CARIBOU

A member of the deer family, there are a number of subspecies of caribou (known as reindeer in Europe), including woodland caribou, that inhabit the remote

Caribou are present in the Maligne Valley, but rarely seen

backcountry of Jasper National Park. Unlike the barrenground caribou, which live in migratory herds of up to 400,000 animals and move enormous distances across the northern tundra, the woodland subspecies spend the summers above the treeline in high alpine areas. Biologists have identified two small herds in the park, including one that is intermittently seen in the Bald Hills and that moves to lower elevations, such as the Maligne Valley, in winter. The name caribou ("hoof scraper") was bestowed on the animal by Aboriginal people for the way they scrape snow off their food with their hooves in the winter. Caribou are smaller than elk and have a dark-brown coat with creamy patches on the neck and rump. Both sexes grow antlers, but those of the females are shorter and have fewer points.

BLACK BEARS

If you spot a bear feeding along Maligne Lake Road, chances are it's a black bear. Although black bears are widespread through all forested areas of the Canadian Rockies, Maligne Lake Road is one of the most reliable places to view them. Their weight varies considerably, but males weigh 150 kilograms (330 pounds) on average and females 100 kilograms (220 pounds). Their diet is omnivorous and consists primarily of grasses and berries, but they supplement this food with small mammals. They are not true hibernators, but in winter they can sleep for up to one month at a time before changing position. During this time, their heartbeats drops to 10 beats per minute, their body temperatures drops, and they lose up to 30 percent of their body weight. Females reach reproductive maturity after five years; cubs are usually born in late winter.

GRIZZLY BEARS

Although grizzlies (also called brown bears) have disappeared from most of North America, they are still widespread throughout

Grizzly bear

the Canadian Rockies—approximately 200–300 live in the region. Grizzlies are often found in remote valleys, although casual observers occasionally spot them in the Maligne Valley. Sightings also occur above the treeline, such as in the Opal Hills; spring and fall are your best chances to see them. The second-largest of eight recognized species of bears (only polar bears are larger), grizzlies (male) on average weigh 200–350 kilograms (440–770 pounds). Its coat ranges from light brown to almost black, with dark tan being the most common colour. Like black bears, grizzlies hibernate through the winter. When they emerge from their dens in spring,

BLACK OR GRIZZLY?

The two species of bears present in the Canadian Rockies—black and grizzly—can be differentiated by size and shape. Grizzlies are larger than black bears and have a flatter, dish-shaped face. Grizzlies also have a distinctive hump of muscle behind their necks. Colour is not a reliable way to tell them apart. Black bears are not always black—they can be brown or cinnamon, which causes people to confuse them with the brown-coloured grizzly.

Black bears are common throughout the Maligne Valley

Marmot habitat ranges from Medicine Lake (pictured) to rockslides high above the treeline

they scavenge the carcasses of animals that succumbed to the winter until the new spring vegetation becomes sufficiently plentiful. The bears eat small- and medium-sized mammals, while in fall, berries make up a large part of their diet.

COYOTES

The coyote is often mistaken for a wolf, when in fact it is much smaller and weighs up to only 15 kilograms (33 pounds). It has a pointed nose and a long, bushy tail. Its colouring is a mottled mix of brown and gray, and its legs and belly are lighter. The coyote is a skillful and crafty hunter that preys mainly on rodents. Coyotes have the remarkable ability to hear the movement of small mammals under the snow, which allows them to hunt these animals without actually seeing them. Coyotes are most commonly seen patrolling the edges of highways and crossing open meadows in low-lying areas, such as the area of the Athabasca River Valley east of the town of Jasper. However, it is not unusual to see coyotes along Maligne Lake Road between Maligne Canyon and Medicine Lake.

WOLVES

Wolves that inhabit the Canadian Rockies are larger than coyotes and larger than the wolves of eastern Canada. They weigh up to 60 kilograms (132 pounds), stand up to one metre (3.2 feet) high at the shoulder, and resemble large huskies or German shepherds. Their colour ranges from snow white to brown or black. They usually hunt in packs of up to eight members that travel, hunt, and rest together. In the pack, these animals adhere to a hierarchical social order. As individuals, they are complex and intriguing, capable of expressing happiness, humour, and loneliness. Once the target of a relentless extermination campaign, the wolf has made an incredible comeback in the Canadian Rockies. Today, over 100 wolves are estimated to roam the region, including a pack that winters in the Maligne Valley.

Red foxes are relatively rare in the Canadian Rockies. This fox caused a traffic jam on Maligne Lake Road.

SMALLER MAMMALS

High above Maligne Lake, hoary marmots are often seen sunning themselves on boulders in rockslides or scampering around alpine meadows (the Bald Hills are a great place to see them). The rocky shoreline of Medicine Lake is also a reliable place to spot them (especially at dusk). Part of the ground squirrel family (as are groundhogs), hoary marmots they are much larger than most squirrels and weigh up to 9 kilograms (19 pounds). When danger approaches, they emit a shrill whistle to warn their colony. Marmots are active only for a few months each summer and spend up to nine months in hibernation every year. The small, greyish pika is a neighbour to the marmot among the rubble and boulders of scree slopes above the treeline.

The bushy-tailed red squirrel, the bold chatterbox of the forest, leaves shelled cones at the base of conifers. The golden-mantled ground squirrel, found in rocky outcrops of subalpine and alpine regions, has black stripes along its sides and looks like an oversized chipmunk.

Birds

Birdwatching is popular in the mountains thanks to the approximately 300 resident species and the millions of migratory birds that pass through the Canadian Rockies each year. Birdwatchers will be enthralled by the diversity of eastern and western bird species that are common in forested areas of the Maligne Valley, such as sparrows, starlings, grouse, ravens, crows, blackbirds, finches, thrushes, hummingbirds, woodpeckers, flycatchers, and warblers. Ptarmigan are common in open meadows above the treeline.

The arrival of the Canada goose to Jasper National Park is a sure sign of spring. By late May, when the ice has melted, they begin congregating on the grassy area in front of the day lodge at Maligne Lake and remain there until fall.

Bald eagles are sometimes seen at Medicine Lake and along the remote shorelines of Maligne Lake in late summer, while migratory golden eagles pass high overhead each spring and fall. Ospreys are another raptor inhabiting the Maligne Valley. They nest high up in dead trees or at the top of utility poles, always in a location overlooking water, where they feed on fish. Due to their nocturnal habits, owls are rarely seen but are widespread through the Canadian Rockies. One resident inhabitant of the Maligne Valley is the northern boreal owl.

Maligne Canyon is one of the few places in the Canadian Rockies where black swifts can be spotted. Slightly larger than a common swallow, these secretive birds nest on narrow ledges of canyon walls, where they are hidden from predators.

CANADA GEESE

Each spring and fall, the skies of western Canada come alive with the honking of the Canada goose, a remarkable bird whose migratory path takes it clear across the continent of North America. Each spring, family units migrate north to the same nesting site year after year. These units are spread throughout the region, from Maligne Lake to desolate islands in the Arctic Ocean. Groups of families migrate together in flocks. Preparation for long flights includes hours of preening and wing flexing. Once in the air, the geese navigate by the sun, moon, and stars. They are intensely aware of air pressure and humidity. In spring, Canada geese hitch a ride north on the strong winds produced by low-pressure systems rolling up from the southwest. In fall, they take advantage of Arctic fronts that roar south. If weather conditions are not right, the geese will rest for a while, usually in fields (where they take advantage of freshly sown crops). The V-formation for which the geese are famous serves a very specific purpose. Each bird positions itself behind and slightly to the side of the bird immediately ahead. In this way, every goose in the flock has a clear view, and all but the leader benefit from the slipstream of the birds ahead.

Canada geese are common along the lakeshore

HARLEQUIN DUCKS

Found on Canada's east and west coasts, harlequin ducks are usually associated with saltwater, although they do migrate short distances to fast-flowing freshwater streams each spring to breed. The harlequins that migrate all the way from the Pacific Ocean to the upper reaches of Maligne River, just below the lake's outlet, are a unique exception to the species. The harlequin's Latin name, Histrionicus, is derived from the Latin word for "stage actor," a reference to the male duck's unique and seemingly painted markings that resemble an actor's make-up. Breeding for the harlequins begins in late May or early June. Their nests are built close to the river; females will stay on the nest for up to a month waiting for her eggs to hatch. The ducklings are able to fly after approximately 40 or 50 days.

Harlequin duck

© Wayne Lynch

Ptarmigan inhabit meadows above the treeline

Maligne Lake, 1924

Past to Present

WORD OF A BEAUTIFUL LAKE KNOWN AS CHABA IMNE (STONEY FOR "BEAVER LAKE") SURROUNDED BY TOWERING MOUNTAINS HAD BEEN PASSED DOWN THROUGH GENERATIONS OF INDIGENOUS PEOPLE, BUT IT WASN'T UNTIL MARY SCHÄFFER REACHED ITS SHORE IN 1908 THAT MALIGNE LAKE BECAME KNOWN TO THE OUTSIDE WORLD.

Since the first tourists were guided to Maligne Lake by Fred Brewster in 1914, the journey has evolved greatly. Instead of a three-day horseback trip, it's now a one-hour drive from downtown Jasper along a paved road, and the handmade wooden boats used a century ago have been replaced by comfortable motorboats that zip up and down the lake.

Sore Foot Lake

Although a fur trading post had been established as early as 1813 in the nearby Athabasca River Valley and Hudson's Bay Company employee Michel Klyne likely visited the lake as early as 1824 on seasonal trading trips to the Kootenay Plains, the first official recording of Maligne Lake was made in 1875 by Henry McLeod (sometimes spelled MacLeod), a railway surveyor. At the time, it had been over six decades since David Thompson had made his historic crossing of Athabasca Pass; the fur trading post in the Athabasca River Valley had been abandoned and the only residents of what

THE WICKED RIVER

The Maligne River was named by Belgian priest Father Pierre-Jean De Smet, who is best remembered for convincing Sioux war chief Sitting Bull to participate in treaty negotiations with the United States government in 1868. Prior to this, he travelled extensively through western North America and ministered to the Native Americans. De Smet's longest journey, which began in 1845, took him up the Columbia River and over White Man Pass on a peace mission involving the Blackfoot Nation. After a summer on the Canadian plains, he spent the winter at Fort Edmonton and then set off for Fort Vancouver via the Athabasca River Valley and Athabasca Pass in the early spring of 1846. During this phase of his trip, De Smet noted the strong current at the confluence of two rivers in his journal and called the waters "maline," a French word for "wicked" or "treacherous." The name "Maligne" was eventually used for not only the river but also for the lake, canyon, pass, mountain, and mountain range.

Father Pierre-Jean De Smet

is now Jasper National Park were a few pioneering families. McLeod was one of 800 men working for Sir Sandford Fleming, assigned by the government to provide the Canadian Pacific Railway (CPR) with reference material as it set out to choose a route for the transcontinental railway. As part of his survey work, McLeod followed the Maligne River to its source but found travelling up the Maligne Valley very difficult—when he reached the lake at the head of the valley, he dubbed it "Sore Foot," for his difficult journey. Not wanting to traverse the valley a second time, McLeod headed east and followed the Rocky River back to the Athabasca River Valley. Not surprisingly, upon returning to Edmonton, McLeod reported to Fleming that the Maligne Valley was not a practical route for the transcontinental railway.

Mary Schäffer

Even 30 years after McLeod's visit, the lake remained a mythical place. Word of its beauty had spread, but it remained remote and difficult to reach. Although the railway was yet to reach Jasper Forest Park, which had been established in 1907, the CPR had been laid across the Canadian Rockies to the south; the settlements of Banff, Lake Louise, Field, and Rogers Pass became popular bases for adventurous travellers, who would hire local guides and head into the wilderness for days or even weeks at a time. One such adventurer was Mary Schäffer, who, like many of her male contemporaries, dedicated her summers to exploring remote regions in the Canadian Rockies. It may be surprising to learn that a woman in the 1900s had been allowed to explore the Canadian wilderness amidst the crude company of packers and guides, and there were likely people who frowned at Schäffer's behaviour. But she did not see how enjoying nature could possibly be equated with indecency, and as a result, she helped to usher in a new era of feminine freedom in a post-Victorian world.

Mary Schäffer

Born Mary Townsend Sharples on October 4, 1861, she grew up in a wealthy, educated, and highly affluent Quaker family from Philadelphia. From a young age, she was encouraged to cultivate her skills in photography and painting. In 1887, 26-year-old Sharples first travelled to the Canadian Rockies along the newly laid CPR with Dr. Charles Schäffer, a friend of Sharples's father, as her chaperone. Although Dr. Schäffer was 23 years older than Sharples, they found kindred spirits in each other, especially when

Samson and Leah Beaver with their daughter Frances Louise

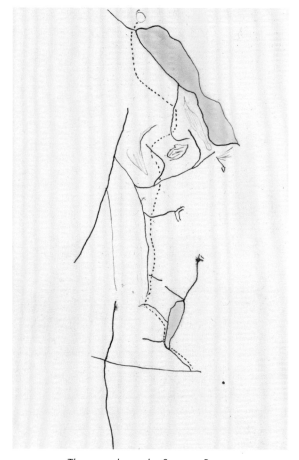

The map drawn by Samson Beaver

it came to their shared love of natural history. Sharples and Dr. Schäffer were married two years later, in 1889. The couple spent most of their summers together exploring the Canadian Rockies until Dr. Schäffer passed away unexpectedly in 1903.

After her husband's death, Schäffer entered a new chapter in her life. In honour of her deceased husband, she returned to the Canadian Rockies in 1904. Banff outfitter Tom Wilson recommended Billy Warren, one of his guides, to lead her through the Canadian wilderness. Over the next few summers, she used her husband's botanical studies to write *Alpine Flora of the Canadian Rockies*, which was published in 1907. After reading *Climbs and Explorations in the Canadian Rockies* (1903), by Hugh Stutfield and John Norman Collie, Schäffer became interested in exploring what lay north of the Columbia Icefield. She was particularly keen to visit Brazeau Lake and search for a lake further north known to the Stoney of the Kootenay Plains as "Chaba Imne" (Beaver Lake).

Returning from a 1907 journey to Brazeau Lake, guides Billy Warren and Sid Unwin led her party to the Kootenay Plains, where their boss, Tom Wilson, had a cabin. At the plains, they were invited to dinner with Wilson's neighbour and fellow outfitter Elliot Barnes. Samson and Leah Beaver and their daughter Frances Louise were also at the dinner. Much of the discussion that night revolved around the North Saskatchewan River Valley, the area from which Schäffer and her party had just returned. When Schäffer spoke of her fascination with the stories she had heard of Chaba Imne, Samson surprised her by saying that not only did he know of the lake but he had visited it as a child with his father. Luckily for Schäffer, Samson remembered the way to the lake and drew her a map. The evening would prove to be momentous for both Schäffer and the history of the Canadian Rockies.

Pushing off from the shoreline aboard the HMS Chaba, *1908*

The following summer, in 1908, Schäffer made an attempt to find the mythical lake. Guided again by Warren and Unwin, she was accompanied by her close friend Mary "Mollie" Adams, botanist Stewardson Brown, a cook, and 22 horses. From the Kootenay Plains, they travelled north over Wilcox Pass to the Sunwapta River and then crossed Poboktan Pass. Travelling by horse usually made things easier, but in her journal, Schäffer wrote of the great difficulty that they had navigating their horses through the densely overgrown trails. The gnarly brush tangled itself around the horses' hooves and made them miserable. The bank of one creek in particular was so bad that Schäffer aptly named it "Tangle Foot."

Regardless of their difficulties, the party eventually reached Maligne Pass. After setting up a camp, Unwin set off, exclaiming, "I'm going to climb something that's high enough to see if that lake's within twenty miles of here, and I'm not coming back until I know!" Then at approximately 10:30 p.m., Unwin appeared through the darkness at camp and shouted, "I've found the lake!" The following morning, the party reached the shore of Chaba Imne. Warren and Unwin set about felling timber to build a raft, which took just one day to build. It was christened HMS *Chaba*, and the entire party paddled out into the heart of the vast body of water known today as Maligne Lake. Schäffer later wrote: " . . . all in our little company agreed, it was

A hand-tinted photograph of Maligne Lake taken on Schäffer's 1908 expedition

the finest view any of us had beheld in the Rockies. This was a tremendous assertion, for, of that band of six of us, and each counted his miles of travel through them by thousands. Yet it lay there, for the time being all ours, —those miles and miles of lake, the unnamed peaks rising above us, one following the other, each more beautiful than the last."

In 1911, by the time Schäffer had published *Old Indian Trails of the Canadian Rockies*, which included a detailed account of her 1908 expedition to Maligne Lake, her fame had spread. At the time, both the government and the Grand Trunk Pacific Railway (GTP) were eager to see Maligne Lake mapped and surveyed so that it could be open to the expected crowds of tourists that would begin arriving by train. Upon the urging of

Donaldson B. Dowling of the Geological Survey of Canada (GSC), Schäffer returned to Maligne Lake in 1911. On this occasion, sponsored by the GTP, she did not travel via the old hunting trails from the south as she had done in 1908 but instead rode the train west from Edmonton to Hinton, or as she described, along the "iron python—an intrusive creature born of an industrial age penetrating deep into once sacred places . . . " Accompanying Schäffer was her sister in-law Caroline Sharples and Caroline's 10-year-old son, Paul.

Of her arrival in Hinton in early June 1911, Schäffer wrote: "Out from the mass of unnumbered nationalities yelled a bona fide bus driver, 'All aboard for Prairie Creek and the Mountain View Hotel!' We saw our tents and blankets and duffle-bag take a flying leap from the baggage van to the waiting mud, and then — O joy! Out of that sea of unknown quantities loomed the familiar face of Jack Otto, our famous old guide from Field, B.C. He was riding a handsome sorrel, and his welcome smile, as he quickly rescued the blankets from the Hinton soil, was worth all the 'Mountain Views' in creation."

From Hinton, Otto guided the Schäffer party west along the Athabasca River passed the distinct peak of Roche Miette and the mining town of Pocahontas before setting up camp at the site of Jasper House, an abandoned fur trading post. The next day they visited with Lewis and Suzette Swift, the lone homesteaders in the valley. Rather than using the Maligne Valley to access Maligne Lake, the government requested that Schäffer survey a trail that had been cut running south from the railway to Buffalo Prairie and then east along Wabasso Creek and up and over the Maligne Range to the north of Curator Mountain. Although snow still covered the trail at higher elevations, Otto guided them to the north shore of Maligne Lake, which they reached on June 19, 1911. Making the journey more difficult was the problem of transporting a rather heavy and cumbersome wooden boat up to the lake. Otto rose to the challenge; he disassembled the boat and tied the planks to the side of his horse. The long planks made it impossible for the horse to navigate its own path, so Jack guided it and used the planks like a rudder to steer.

Maligne Lake was to be Schäffer's home for the next six weeks. And while her cheery description of their camp suggests an easy and idyllic vacation, there was work to be done. Using a compass, Schäffer began surveying the lake. She later wrote, "It did not take more than two days' work for me to realize it was no child's play, or the work a matter of a few days." Mary and her crew worked from north to south, taking measurements to create a

SHOVEL PASS

Jack Otto crossing Shovel Pass with wooden planks that were used to build a boat once Maligne Lake was reached by the 1911 Schäffer party.

In the spring of 1911, in anticipation of Mary Schäffer's survey of Maligne Lake, a trail starting from the Athabasca River at Buffalo Prairie was cut through the Maligne Range. When the government-contracted workers—which included Jasper guides Bruce and Closson Otto—reached a snow-covered pass below Curator Mountain, they fashioned shovels from nearby spruce trees to dig a path through the snow. Today, the pass is known as Shovel Pass, which is also the name of a backcountry lodge along the trail. The original crude wooden shovels can be viewed at the Jasper Yellowhead Museum.

survey that was used to create the first official government map of Maligne Lake. As part of her submission to the government, Schäffer suggested names for many of the surrounding geological features, including mounts Warren and Unwin for her guides and Samson and Leah peaks for her Stoney friends. For the peak beside Unwin, Schäffer proposed Mount Charlton, for Harry Ready Charlton, GTP publicity agent who had sponsored her expedition. As was the toponymic standard, Schäffer chose to name Maligne Lake for the river it fed. All names were approved by November 1911.

MOUNT WARREN

One of the highest mountains in the Maligne Lake area is the 3,362-metre (11,030-foot) Mount Warren, at its remote south end. William "Billy" Warren guided Mary Schäffer throughout the Canadian Rockies, and their travels took them to the shore of Maligne Lake in 1908. When Schäffer first saw the mountain upon which she bestowed her guide's name, she described it as "massive and dignified"—two qualities that she associated with Warren's kind and generous nature.

Billy Warren (right)

Warren, like many of the earliest guides in the Canadian Rockies, was originally from England. He was born at Harlow, Essex, in 1880. In 1899, he joined the Imperial Yeomanry and served throughout the duration of the Boer War. Warren then crossed the Atlantic Ocean in search of adventure in the wilds of western Canada. Arriving in Banff in 1903, he found employment with outfitter Tom Wilson. After one season as a wrangler, he was promoted to the position of guide. Warren's first client was Schäffer, and their relationship evolved into marriage in June 1915.

By 1919, Warren foresaw automobiles as the future of mountain travel. He opened a garage on Banff's main street and then converted an old livery into Rocky Mountain Tours & Transport (now home to Banff's famous Grizzly House restaurant). Although he remains best known for his historic link to Maligne Lake, Warren's career shift from trail guide to businessman proved to be a wise one, and he sealed his place as one of Banff's most successful businessmen.

The house Billy Warren built for Mary Schäffer in Banff

Early Guiding

In 1911, four years after Jasper Forest Park had been established, the Department of the Interior created a Dominion Parks Branch, and James Bernard Harkin was selected as commissioner. Harkin believed that a park should not be maintained merely for its wilderness; he wrote that parks should be created so that "every citizen of Canada may satisfy his soul-craving for nature and nature's beauty; that he may absorb the energy and power of the sunshine and the fresh air; that nature's smiles may be reflected into him and that he may sing with the wind and laugh with mountain torrents."

Before Harkin was appointed, and even before the first passenger trains began rolling into the divisional point of Fitzhugh (now the town of Jasper), a number of guides and outfitters had established businesses in the park in anticipation of a tourism boom. The Moberly brothers, born in the Athabasca River Valley, were joined by the Brewsters, the Ottos, the Hargreaves, and Curly Phillips—all of whom played an important role in Jasper's development as a tourist destination. They combined a love of adventure with a flair for business, sensing the park's potential as an opportunity to do business with those who were looking for adventure in the Canadian Rockies.

One of Jasper's best-known outfitters was Frederick Archibald Brewster, who was born in Kildonan, Manitoba, in 1884. His parents, John and Isabella Brewster, moved west from Manitoba in 1888 and established a dairy to provide milk for the Banff Springs Hotel. After earning an engineering degree from Queen's University in Ontario, Fred and his younger brother, Jack, arrived in the Athabasca River Valley in the spring of 1911. After spending a year working for the GTP, which was being constructed through the valley, the two brothers had enough money to start their own guiding business. Along with their brother-in-law, Phil Moore, Fred and Jack established Brewster and Moore's in 1912. Fred was a voracious reader of early literature regarding the Canadian Rockies, which made him a favourite with scientific expeditions looking for knowledgeable locals; he also

THE OTHER BREWSTER BROTHERS

While the name Fred Brewster is well known in Jasper, it was his two older brothers, Bill and Jim, who began the business that grew to become the Brewster company, which operates the fleet of Ice Explorer buses on the Columbia Icefield and the Brewster tour buses seen throughout the Canadian Rockies.

In 1892, Jim and Bill Brewster, at ages 10 and 12 respectively, were hired by the Banff Springs Hotel to take guests to local landmarks. As their reputation as guides grew, they built a thriving business. By 1900, they had their own livery and outfitting company, and soon thereafter they expanded operations to Lake Louise. Their other early business interests included a trading post, the original Mount Royal Hotel in Banff, the first ski lodge in the Sunshine Meadows, and a chalet at the Columbia Icefield.

Jim Brewster

Renowned Western artist Alexander Phimister Proctor painting at Maligne Lake, 1911

guided big game hunters and wealthy tourists who arrived on the newly completed railway. During this time, he visited Maligne Lake a number of times and travelled along a rough trail running up the Rocky River and through the Colin Range via Jacques Lake.

Before the onset of World War I, Fred Brewster and a crew of local men were contracted by the government to clear a wagon road up the Maligne Valley as far as Medicine Lake. It ran along the base of Old Fort Point, past Tent City (now Jasper Park Lodge), and between Lakes Edith and Annette before switchbacking up to the top of Maligne Canyon.

Brewster subsequently established tent camps at the south end of Medicine Lake and the north end of Maligne Lake. Guests travelled by horseback from the Athabasca River Valley up the Maligne Valley on the wagon road and then along Medicine Lake to a junction with an old trail that led down from Jacques Lake. Arriving at the south end of Medicine Lake, tourists were accommodated in primitive tent cabins, which comprised a planked floor and log walls covered with canvas. Two tents were set up for sleeping and a third for dining. From Medicine Lake, it was a full day's horseback ride to Maligne Lake, where a similar cluster of tent cabins overlooked the north end of lake. The first guests—Josephine Rathbone, a well-travelled librarian from New York, and a young man from the Curtis Publishing Company and his wife—arrived at Brewster's Maligne Lake camp in 1914. At this time, the camp hosted a maximum of four guests at any one time, plus two camp attendants. The raft left behind by Schäffer in 1911 was used to take guests out onto the lake.

Grace Phillips with son Sam, who was born in 1928

Curly Phillips in the 1930s

In 1915, Brewster volunteered for military service in World War I. Commissioned as a major, he served with distinction with the 2nd Tunnelling Company of the Canadian Engineers in England and France. He was awarded the Military Cross on January 1, 1917, and returned to Jasper in 1919.

Another of the earliest guiding and outfitting businesses based in Jasper Forest Park was operated by Donald Nelson "Curly" Phillips, nicknamed for his curly locks. He was born on April 15, 1884, in Dorset, Ontario. Curly's father, Daniel Alvin Phillips, was responsible for giving Curly an early start at outdoor education. By the age of 12, Curly was already managing his own trapline. He was also a master craftsman of boats, a skill he had learned under his father's guidance. It was a combination of these skills and his confidence that made Curly one of the park's most sought-after guides.

Curly arrived in the Athabasca River Valley in 1909, at the beginning of a new age of exploration. The timing was perfect on his part—the first thing an explorer required was a competent guide and someone to outfit him or her for the wilderness. Curly gained a reputation for being reliable, remaining calm in all types of unpredictable situations, and protecting his clients from wild animals. He also mastered the use of an axe—a prized quality in a road-less park with few trails. His skill was exceptional when it came to building canoes, cabins, and temporary bridges across rivers.

Curly was also endorsed by the Alpine Club of Canada as one of its official outfitters, which was a huge boast for business. In the summer of 1911, Curly outfitted a joint Alpine Club of Canada–Smithsonian Institution expedition to the Mount Robson region that included such luminaries as Austrian mountaineer Conrad Kain; surveyor Arthur O. Wheeler; George Kinney, who is best known for

In the 1920s, the Dominion Parks Branch hired professional photographers to produce images showing the beauty of Canada's parks, including this photo by William Oliver.

his Mount Robson summit attempts; and palaeontologist Dr. Charles Walcott, who is credited with discovering the Burgess Shale in Yoho National Park. After returning from Robson, Curly and James Shand-Harvey, an Eton-educated guide who settled in the park around the same time as Curly, led the party to Maligne Lake along the same trail from Buffalo Prairie used by Schäffer earlier that year. Accompanying the party was artist Alexander Phimister Proctor and photographer, Byron Harmon, of Banff. Using a large format camera, Harmon's negatives from this 1911 trip produce black and white prints of exceptional quality.

At the conclusion of the 1924 summer guiding season, Curly married Grace Inkster, whom he had met at a skating party in Edmonton. Inkster was a member of a pioneering family who had homesteaded the King Edward Park area, southeast of downtown, as early as the 1870s. The couple had three children: Sam (born in 1928), Joy (1930), and Ivy (1932).

Even after World War I, the wagon road up the Maligne Valley was very rough and ended well before Maligne Lake, but it did open up the valley to more visitors. These visitors included Lawren Harris and Alexander Young Jackson, in 1924. Two of Canada's well-known Group of Seven painters, they were contracted by the Canadian National Railway (CNR) to produce paintings of the park. With wardens transporting their ample

Lawren S. Harris. Maligne Lake, Jasper Park, 1924

art supplies up the Maligne Valley, the two artists established a lakeside base camp and then travelled the length of the lake by boat and hiked into the surrounding hills in search of artistic panoramas. During this trip, Harris painted Maligne Lake in his recognizable simple, decorative style; he used cold shades of blue and turquoise to illustrate the solitude of the wilderness. This historic piece of art is now owned by the National Gallery of Canada.

Byron Harmon, who had visited Maligne Lake in 1911 as the official photographer of an Alpine Club of Canada–Smithsonian Institution expedition, returned in 1924. On this occasion, he was accompanied by Lewis Freeman, an explorer and travel writer with over a dozen books to his credit. The writer and photographer teamed up to complete the most comprehensive photographic record of the Canadian Rockies ever assembled. They were guided by "Soapy" Smith, who took his name from a famous Klondike conman. The party also included a horse wrangler, a cook, and 16 horses to help transport a significant amount of photographic equipment. The epic 70-day, 800-kilometre (500-mile) trip through the Columbia Icefield and Athabasca River Valley began in Lake Louise and travelled as far north as Jasper. Beginning their return journey from Jasper on October 2, 1924, the party travelled south up the Maligne Valley to Maligne Lake, where they camped for three days. In his 1925 book, *On the Roof of the Rockies*, which tells the story of the expedition, Freeman waxed lyrically about Maligne Lake: "The view up the lake from a high point half a mile above the Narrows, with a slender timbered peninsula in the foreground, the sparkling emerald waters in the middle distance, and snow-crowned mountain peaks and the blue-green ice of hanging glaciers reared against a vault of sapphire sky for a background, is one of the most perfect settings of its kind on the continent."

The following year, in 1925, the Trail Riders of the Canadian Rockies—supported by luminaries such as Mary Schäffer, Commissioner of Dominion Parks J.B. Harkin, artist Carl Rungius, and Fred Brewster's older brothers Jim and Bill—had its annual powwow at Maligne Lake.

In addition to guiding, Fred and Jack Brewster were involved in the original Jasper Park Lodge, which is regarded today as one of the world's premier mountain resorts. Before World War I, the lodging comprised canvas tents spread along the shore of Lac Beauvert (then known as Horseshoe Lake), across the Athabasca River from the railway, and was known as Tent City. In 1921, the brothers sold Tent City to the CNR, which was anxious to establish a flagship resort that could compete with CPR resorts like the Banff Springs. Despite selling Tent City, the Brewsters retained exclusive rights to operate trail rides. Brewster trail rides and overnight trips up the Maligne Valley to the two camps were often featured in railway advertising and other publications. As a result, Fred Brewster's Rocky Mountain Camps became extremely popular. Meanwhile, Jack had begun offering three-week pack trips along the Glacier Trail,

which ran from Jasper to Lake Louise via Maligne Lake and Maligne Pass.

In 1927, Fred Brewster complemented his tent cabins by adding a log chalet, and the following year, a log chalet was added to his Medicine Lake camp. By the mid-1920s, the golden era of guiding was coming to an end in the Canadian Rockies, so Curly Phillips sought employment as Brewster's Maligne Lake camp manager. In addition to his duties around the chalet, Curly spent his time building a boat. He had built his first boat for Brewster in 1920, but this one was larger and would be the first with a motor to be used on Maligne Lake. Six metres (20-feet) long and seating 24 passengers, it

AZALEA ADAMS

Azalea Adams grew up in New York during the early years of the last century and enjoyed a childhood of wealth and privilege. But in 1919 she was swept off her feet by handsome Canadian soldier Fred Brewster, who regularly visited New York to promote his Jasper camps. Upon his return from World War I, they were quietly married she returned to Jasper with Brewster in 1924. According to an article in a 1926 edition of Canadian National Railway Magazine, the young socialite adapted well to the remote Canadian Rockies—Brewster built her an impressive log home on the edge of the Jasper townsite, showed her how to cook on the trail, and taught her wilderness survival skills.

In 1928, however, in her mid-30s and after living in Jasper for only a few years, Adams suffered a nervous breakdown. It was an era when mental disorders and depression were not widely discussed, so little is known about her later years except that she passed away in 1961 at a psychiatric hospital in Quebec. Brewster brought her body back to Jasper so she could be buried in Jasper Cemetery. The couple did not have any children, and Fred Brewster never remarried.

could easily reach Samson Narrows (Spirit Island) in a few hours, something that had not been possible in the past.

The scenic cruises proved so popular that Curly applied for his own tour boat concession. After being granted permission, he set to work building a boathouse along the same stretch of lakeshore as the Brewster dock. It was supported by log pilings driven into the shallow water at the lakeshore with planked decking. The actual building was of post-and-beam construction; it was 12 metres (40 feet) wide and 15 metres (50 feet) long and topped by a shingle roof. Completed in 1929, the structure was entirely in keeping with the government's architectural guidelines and remains an iconic building to this day.

Soon after opening the boathouse, Curly built the cedar-planked *Leah*, which was named for

MALIGNE LAKE CHALET

The heart of Fred Brewster's Rocky Mountain Camp was Maligne Lake Chalet, which opened in 1927 on a slight rise at the north end of the lake. Although it was completed long before there was road access to the outside world, it was one of the few places—aside from the Jasper Park Lodge and a few hotels in downtown Jasper—offering tourist accommodations in the park.

Fitting perfectly with the government's aesthetic vision for architecture within the park, the structure was a single-storey building of horizontal logs with a gabled roof. Overnight guests were accommodated in adjacent tent cabins, and the chalet contained a dining room, kitchen, and communal living space. In 1935, Brewster expanded his Maligne Lake operation by

The adjacent guesthouse opened in 1935

adding an additional four-bedroom guesthouse. According to historical records from 1935, he also applied for a permit to build a covered veranda on the chalet and a separate building to house bathroom facilities.

Maligne Lake Chalet remained in use until 1976, when the adjacent Maligne Tours day lodge was completed. Over the next decade, it was used sporadically as a recreation room for Maligne Tours staff. As a government-owned building of historic importance, it was added to the Register of the Government of Canada Heritage Buildings in 1988. Today, after extensive restoration undertaken by Maligne Tours, the beautiful log building stands as a tribute to Fred Brewster and his considerable contributions to early tourism at the lake.

Interior of the chalet

the wife of Samson Beaver, who had drawn the map that helped Schäffer find the lake two decades previously. The boat remained in service until the 1970s. Twelve passengers could be seated on the wooden bench that ran down the centre of the boat; blankets were offered on cooler days.

At the same time Curly was building his boathouse, the government began stocking Maligne Lake with trout. This attracted anglers—a new breed of visitors who were anxious to rent boats. They rented boats from Curly for $0.50 for the first hour and $0.25 for each hour after or at a flat rate of $2.00 per day. By this time, Curly had erected simple tent cabins near his boathouse, which offered accommodation and food for up to 25 guests at one time at what he advertised as Rainbow Camp. His brother (Harry), his father (Alvin), his brother-in-law (Bert Wilkins), as well as Jasper locals such as Adam Joachim, who was a descendant of one of the region's first fur traders, helped him run his camp. The earliest promotional brochures for Curly's Rainbow Camp boasted of fishing, boating, summer skiing, and mountain climbing.

When Brewster first established his camp at Maligne Lake in 1914, visitors travelled by horseback all the way from the Athabasca River Valley to Maligne Lake. After World War I, when the wagon road was widened to accommodate automobile traffic, the journey was shortened considerably. From the end of the road at the north end of Medicine Lake, Brewster and Curly Phillips began transporting their guests by boat to the south end of Medicine Lake, where they would spend the night. The following morning, they saddled up for a trail ride between Medicine and Maligne lakes. Although it still took two days to reach Maligne Lake, the trip was a popular adventure with tourists from around the world; Brewster offered the option of returning to the Athabasca River Valley and Jasper townsite via Shovel Pass and Buffalo

Nick Bleskie was one of Fred Brewster's most trusted guides

Prairie (the route taken by Schäffer in 1911). This "circle trip" had been pioneered by Brewster as early as 1914.

In 1933, Brewster and one of his cowboys, Charlie Bowlen, ventured north of Shovel Pass in the hopes of finding a more scenic return route to Jasper than crossing the Maligne Range to Buffalo Prairie, which was the traditional route taken on his circle trips. The route they found, along the slopes of Mount Tekarra, linked to trail leading to the summit of Signal Mountain; the trail had been used by Morrison P. Bridgland in 1915 during his survey of the park. After four years of trail building, the link was completed, which created a spectacular trail routed mostly high above the treeline between the Athabasca River Valley and Maligne Lake. Known today as the Skyline Trail, the first two guests recorded to have completed the new route were two young women, Louise Bryant of Montana and

Grace Hartzell of Los Angeles, California. Upon their return to town, tourists were issued a commemorative certificate signed by Brewster, which declared that they were members of the "fellowship of the select company of the riders of the Skyline Trail, Jasper National Park."

Horses were an integral part of transporting both supplies and tourists to Maligne Lake. At the beginning of each summer season, Brewster and Phillips would hire wranglers to look after their precious horses. The hired hands were also expected to cook, help maintain the camp buildings, and take tourists on extended trail rides. Nick Bleskie was typical of the cowboys hired by Brewster. Born in Manitoba in 1896, Bleskie headed west at just 11 years old. By the mid-1930s, he found himself working for Brewster at Maligne Lake; he worked as a guide and boatman and tended horses. Bleskie became renowned in Jasper for his rapport with horses, especially with a horse named Bluebell, who used to give him kisses.

THE HARRAGIN SISTERS

While names such as Brewster, Otto, and Phillips are well known in Jasper, few people have heard of Agnes and Mona Harragin, the first female guides to be licensed in Jasper National Park. Agnes and Mona were born in 1904 and 1906 respectively, in Port au Spain, Trinidad, and moved to Canada as young children. Barely out of their teens, the two plucky girls found employment managing Fred Brewster's camp at Medicine Lake in 1927. The following summer, they were keen to begin guiding, as Agnes's diary entry shows:

Agnes (top right) and Mona (bottom left) adapted well to life as guides

. . . Of course the beginning of 1928 stands out in my memory because I was starting on a new job in a new location. In the early spring of that year, I received a letter from Brewster's office offering the job of cook and hostess to Mona and me, also giving us the privilege of choosing any Brewster camp in the park . . . Both of us did a great deal of thinking with Mona finally suggesting that we just simply write back saying that, unless we could guide, we would not be returning to Jasper for the tourist season. Secretly we decided that, if we were refused, we would write back immediately accepting the previous offer, picking Maligne Lake camp. I will never forget my inward feelings when a reply came back stating that both of us would be hired on as guides for the "Circle Trip," with our base camp at Medicine Lake . . . Incidentally, later in that year, I learned that Mrs. Brewster had insisted that girls should be given a trial run on guiding because, she for one, would far rather make the round trip with one of her own kind as guide. She suggested that a number of other women would be of the same opinion.

In 1928, they were indeed issued licences to guide guests between Jasper and Maligne Lake. In 1930, Agnes married Mark Truxler, another Brewster guide, and Mona married Charlie Matheson, a park warden. Agnes and Mark lived for many years in the railway station at Old Entrance, just outside the eastern park boundary. For a time, they managed Miette Hot Springs and were then employed as caretakers at Jasper's East Park Gate. Mona and Charlie operated a trail riding operation in Jasper until 1940, when they established Circle M Guest Ranch, just outside the park's east gate. Today, Mona Lake, a short walk from Maligne Lake, is named in the younger sister's honour.

Winter Wonderland

Although sports such as skiing and snowboarding are popular throughout the Canadian Rockies to this day, Maligne Lake remains quiet throughout the winter. The first recorded ski trip to Maligne Lake was undertaken in 1922 by park warden Pete Withers and Jasper locals Vern and Doug Jeffery. During the week-long adventure, they skied up the Maligne Valley as far as the Bald Hills, detoured to Jacques Lake, and also reached the summit of Evelyn Pass in the Maligne Range. Two years later, the three men, along with Fred Brewster, founded the Jasper Ski Club. Although the club focused on events around the town, its more adventurous members regularly skied into the Maligne Valley; Withers later wrote, "Based on the combined experience of these trips, covering a period which includes twelve winters, the general consensus of opinion is that the stretch of country from Maligne Lake, (including the Shovel Pass and Little Shovel) over the [Henry] McLeod Glacier to the Poboktan Summit and Jonas Shoulder gives a better combination of good qualities than any other country skied over. It includes every kind of slope from the 'nursery' variety at the lower end of Maligne Lake to the 1000-foot slopes of the [Henry] McLeod Glacier, and has the advantage of being a direct winter route to the Icefield and Banff."

The popularity of skiing in the Maligne Valley brought about the formation of the Maligne Lake Ski Club in the 1930s. In 1936, four of its most active members—the Jeffery brothers, Curly Phillips, and Swiss-born Joe Weiss—built a log cabin high above Maligne Lake near Shovel Pass at a location that became known as Snowbowl, for its abundant snow. The Maligne Lake Ski Club began offering guided ski trips to their cabin, which was known as "Shangri-La." The adventure cost $30 and included a week of lodging,

By the 1930s, ski trips into the Maligne Valley became popular

meals, and transportation from town to Medicine Lake.

Unfortunately, it was Curly's love of skiing that lead to his death. In 1938, aged 54, he and two school-aged brothers, Alan and Reginald Pugh, set out for Elysium Pass in search of a location to build another cabin. As they approached the pass, Alan stopped to adjust his skis while Curly and Reginald continued forward. In a matter of seconds, the tracks ahead of Alan disappeared in a silent but swift avalanche. Alan later wrote, "The slide came off Elysium Mountain in a main body, approximately 300 yards wide, catching both Curly and Reg. After the slide stopped, I went back to look for them, but found no trace. I called but received no answer."

Word quickly spread throughout Jasper that there had been an avalanche and that Curly and one of the Pugh boys were missing. The town immediately banded together; search parties were sent out and other people stayed behind to comfort Curly's wife and family. The search lasted a week before Reginald's body was recovered, and another week went by before Curly's body was found. Famed mountaineer J. Monroe Thorington wrote the

Maligne Lake Chalet, winter 1940

following tribute, which was published in the *American Alpine Journal*: "Curly is remembered as a man of quiet reserve always ready to laugh, as one who moved like a shadow in the woods, and carved his own brand of woodsmanship out of old Indian ways and his own integrity as a person who relied on himself. These are the qualities for which the man and his times should be remembered for these are the strengths modern people need most." Mount Phillips, on the Continental Divide between Jasper National Park and Mount Robson Provincial Park, is named in his honour.

In 1939, Fred Brewster began opening Maligne Lake Chalet for winter visitors. Enthusiastic about the new venture at the end of the winter season, he wrote:

"We feel that we have completed a most successful season. It was our first year in handling tourist skiers and the result of our work has given us great encouragement for success next season. We have worked out an efficient system of transportation and we are able to take people from either train, westbound No. 1 or the eastbound No. 2 and put them into Maligne Lake Chalet that same day. This is accomplished by three types of transportation. Automobile from the station to Medicine Lake, across Medicine Lake in a snowmobile, where team and sleigh wait to take them to Maligne Lake Chalet . . . We have accommodation at Maligne Lake Chalet for forty ski guests. Excellent and healthful meals, including fresh meat and vegetables are served at all times. The buildings are warm and comfortable and an efficient and cheerful staff is in charge there. Our rates for the past season were as low as we could possibly manage - $5.00 a day and $32.00 a week, including transportation and accommodation."

Looking down to frozen Maligne Lake from the Bald Hills in 1947

The Modern Era

At the onset of World War II, the government employed conscientious objectors (Canadian men who refused military service, mostly due to religion) to work on numerous road projects in Jasper National Park. Completion of the Jasper–Banff Highway (Icefields Parkway) was their main task, but the men also upgraded the road between Maligne Canyon and Medicine Lake, built the road out to Sixth Bridge on the lower Maligne River, and constructed a rough fire road between Medicine and Maligne lakes. Even after the road up the Maligne Valley had been upgraded, the section between Maligne Canyon and the end of the road at Medicine Lake was a narrow track designated as one-way. Vehicles heading towards Medicine Lake were allowed to enter during even hours; those travelling back to town were only permitted on the road during odd hours. There was a gatekeeper posted at Maligne Canyon to monitor the traffic.

While there was a slight drop in the number of visitors travelling to Jasper during World War II, Brewster's Maligne Lake Chalet remained a popular spot for tourists; in 1940, Brewster wrote that he hosted a record 131 guests. He also remarked that an increase in guests had made it difficult for his packers to keep up with the amount of supplies needed. In order to make the transportation of supplies easier, Brewster employed a crew of men to widen the trail between Medicine and Maligne lakes; although the original horse trail was more like a road after his men worked on it, it was still barely wide enough to accommodate a vehicle. Brewster then rafted a fleet of old Packard touring cars across Medicine Lake and began using them to transport guests and supplies between Medicine and Maligne lakes. With the vehicles in place, travel time between the Jasper townsite and Maligne Lake was reduced to eight hours. Travel time was reduced even

The road between Medicine and Maligne Lakes, 1947

Tent cabins were the main accommodation at Maligne Lake

further as Brewster made improvements to the road over the next decade.

After Curly's untimely death in 1938, his wife, Grace, took over Rainbow Camp. Larry and Hilda Magistad were employed as managers; the couple ran the tent camp, rented canoes and rowboats, and operated boat tours out of Curly's boathouse aboard the *Leah*. For eight years, Grace remained involved with Curly's business while raising their three children by herself. In 1946, she sold Rainbow Camp to Jack and Colin McIsaac, Roy Olberg, Lyle Johnson, and Harry Alexander. Although Grace eventually moved back to Edmonton, Curly and Grace's son, Sam, continued to work at the lake as a fishing guide.

The new owners renamed the business "Rainbow Tours" and opened a ticket office in downtown Jasper at Joe Weiss's Tekarra Gift Shop at 607 Patricia Street. In 1947, Rainbow Tours began using specially designed seven-passenger Dodge vehicles to transport their guests between Medicine and Maligne lakes.

The following year, they constructed Rainbow Lodge. Located on the site of today's Maligne Tours day lodge, it was similar in function to Brewster's adjacent Maligne Lake Chalet—designed as a place for day-trippers and overnight guests to dine and relax. In 1948, the heated Rainbow Tours tent cabins, which were advertised as having "spring beds," rented for $8.00 per person per day, inclusive of transportation from Jasper and all meals. It cost $15.00 to rent a powered canoe for a full day and $3.50 for a rowboat. It was possible to make a day trip to Maligne Lake from the Jasper Park Lodge or the Jasper townsite, but it was a long day, as the tour departed at 8:00 a.m. and did not return until 8:00 p.m. that evening.

After the summer season of 1952, Rainbow Tours was purchased by Neil Campbell, an Edmonton businessman, who changed the name of the company to the more appropriate "Maligne Tours." In 1955, after just three years, Campbell sold Maligne Tours to Bill Ruddy, who had pioneered snowcat

BILL RUDDY

Born in Hanna, Alberta, in 1924, Bill Ruddy moved to Jasper in 1945, after serving three years in the Royal Canadian Navy. In 1948, Ruddy married Evelyn Hargreaves, the daughter of Jasper pioneers John Albert (Jack) and Gladys Hargreaves. Jack was one of Jasper's original outfitters and had begun working as a wrangler for the Otto brothers in 1914. He later established an outfitting business with his three brothers at Mount Robson before returning to Jasper in 1923.

Bill and Evelyn Ruddy had four children—Gordon, Russell, and twin girls Maureen and Susan. When Ruddy first arrived in Jasper, he worked for the railway, as his father had done. Not finding the work to his liking, he tried a number of different jobs in town, including a job as a government health inspector. Eventually, in 1952, with business partner Tom McCready, he purchased a tracked passenger Snowcat from Bombardier and began offering tours on the Columbia Icefield. In the winters, the two men used the same vehicles to transport skiers to the top of ski runs at Marmot Basin.

Bill Ruddy in 1966, a few years after purchasing Maligne Tours

In addition to his long relationship with Maligne Lake, Ruddy was instrumental in the development of the Marmot Basin ski area, helped scout a location for the Jasper Tramway, served three terms as president of the Jasper Chamber of Commerce, and still found time to teach Sunday school at Jasper's United Church.

tours on the Columbia Icefield. Bill and his wife Evelyn were renowned for their hands-on approach to ensuring that visitors to Maligne Lake enjoyed themselves, and they were equally popular with their staff members, many of whom returned year after year. They built wooden guest cabins beside the existing tent cabins and constructed a new washroom building (now the Maligne Tours ticket office). Ruddy was known for his distinctive outfit—green woollen pants and shirt and a Bavarian-style green alpine hat with a feather. (Staff liked to recite, "The man in the green who runs the scene at Maligne.") In 1959, Ruddy built a ticket office in downtown Jasper at 414 Connaught Drive. Known today as the Maligne Building, it was constructed with

distinctive pink-tinged rock from the Jonas Slide, an ancient rock slide crossed by the Icefields Parkway around 75 kilometres (47 miles) south of town.

Also changing hands during this era was the iconic Brewster's Rocky Mountain Camps, which was purchased by Tom and Yvette Vinson in 1955. Tom Vinson had worked as a wrangler for Brewster since arriving in Jasper in 1939 and had met his future wife while she was working at the Jasper Park Lodge. The Vinsons' main interests were trail riding and backcountry pack trips, so when they purchased the company Brewster had owned and operated for over four decades, the Maligne Lake camp was excluded from the sale. Seven years later, Brewster sold the Maligne Lake camp to Calgarian Ken Lucas, who owned it for seven years before selling to Bill Ruddy.

With the completion of the Yellowhead Highway imminent, joining Maligne Lake by road to the outside world became a priority in the 1960s. By 1965, a rough road had been built all the way to Maligne Lake, but it was only open to the public as far as the south end of Medicine Lake, from where buses shuttled visitors by bus to Maligne Lake. With a road completed, boat service across Medicine Lake was discontinued and Brewster's original Medicine Lake Chalet, built where the Maligne River flows into Medicine Lake, was dismantled log by log and moved to the Vinson's Rocky Mountain Ranch, east of Jasper National Park.

It was not only tourists visiting the lake; Jasper locals would leave their boats at the lake all summer and would ride the bus to get to the boats, which were mostly used for fishing. In 1967, as the road beyond Medicine Lake was further improved, the public parking area was moved further

south. Finally, in 1969, the public road was completed all the way to Maligne Lake and then paved the following summer. Another major change that took place at Maligne Lake in the 1960s was the closure of tourist accommodations, as had been mandated in a 1963 government report (although tent cabins remained at the lake as staff accommodations until 1985).

On March 4, 1969, Fred Brewster, who had come to be known as "Mr. Jasper," passed away in an Edmonton hospital, aged 85. He had officially retired many years earlier, after selling his business to Vinson in 1955. Up until his death, he remained very active in the Jasper community. He was a founding member of the Jasper–Yellowhead Historical Society and was honoured as a life member of the Jasper Ski Club, the Jasper Chamber of Commerce and the Jasper branch of the Canadian Legion. Major Fred Brewster is buried in the Jasper cemetery next to his wife, Azalea.

In anticipation of a flood of visitors arriving in their own vehicles after Maligne Lake Road opened to the public, Ruddy

Rainbow Lodge was completed in 1948

Fred Brewster (left) in 1959, four years after selling his Maligne Lake business

purchased additional tour boats and, in 1977, constructed the present-day lodge on the site of the Rainbow Lodge. During this time, Ruddy converted the four-bedroom guesthouse Brewster had built in 1935 into a residence for himself, his wife, and their two daughters; his two sons bunked in the upper level of today's ticket office. In 1980, after almost three decades at Maligne Lake, Ruddy sold Maligne Tours to Gerry Levasseur.

Unlike today, there were few restrictions on visitors to Maligne Lake up until the 1970s, even after the road had been completed and tourists were arriving by the thousands by automobile. In an effort to protect the lake from fuel spills and noisy boats, gasoline-powered boats were banned in the 1970s; only battery-charged electric motors were permitted and the ban still holds to this day (Maligne Tours is granted an exemption and is allowed to power its tour boats with Volvo Penta engines driving twin propellers). Additionally, travel by all motorboats was restricted to the northern half of the lake. In the 1970s, there was interest in building a large marina and two lakeside motels; it was even proposed that a road should be built across Maligne Pass to create a direct route between Maligne Lake and the Icefields Parkway. Although none of these grandiose plans came to fruition, an impressive bridge was built across the outlet of Maligne Lake in preparation for the road over Maligne Pass that never eventuated.

As the number of visitors to Maligne Lake continued to increase into the 1980s, so

Before a road was completed to Maligne Lake, Fred Brewster and Curly Phillips established adjacent docks at the north end of Medicine Lake (opposite, top) from where tourists would take a boat ride to the south end of the lake and be transferred to vehicles (opposite, bottom) for the final leg of the journey to Maligne Lake.

MALIGNE LAKE WARDENS

Beginning as early as 1909, wardens—originally known as "fire and game guardians"—were dispatched throughout what was then Jasper Forest Park (Jasper officially became a national park in 1930) to ensure park rules and regulations were being followed. They travelled by horseback and stayed in cabins scattered across the backcountry. The earliest warden cabins were very primitive and were usually built by the wardens themselves with locally harvested timber.

According to research conducted by Mike Wesbrook, Ed McDonald was the first documented warden assigned to the Maligne district. It is believed that McDonald built a lakeside cabin in 1919 somewhere near what is now known as Picnic Point (just beyond the boathouse). McDonald was followed by John Weston Macklin, who held the post until 1932; he was replaced by Charlie Matheson, who lived at the lake with his wife Mona, the guide for whom Mona Lake is named. (Since the couple left the lake in 1937, there has been a lack of records regarding the resident warden.) Bert Langston was the Maligne Lake warden from 1947 until 1949, when he was replaced by Mickey McGuire, who was born and raised in Jasper. McGuire and his wife Rosetta lived at Maligne Lake until 1951, after which McGuire was promoted to chief park warden, a position he held for 20 years. He was replaced at the lake by his brother, Larry, who was stationed at Maligne Lake until 1958. By 1954, Larry had completed a more elaborate warden residence at Boathouse Bay. As there was no road access, living at Maligne Lake was challenging for warden families. The challenges led to regular turnover through the 1960s: Anton (Toni) Klettl and his wife Shirley (1958–1960); George and Effie Wells (1960–1964) and Mac and Kathy Elder (1964–1972).

By the time Elder took over the Maligne Lake station in the mid-1960s, the focus of Parks

Charlie Matheson, Maligne Lake warden from 1932 to 1937

Canada was changing. Rather than simply ensuring visitor enjoyment and safety, the organization and its wardens began attempting to create a balance between tourism and the environment. Previously, at Maligne Lake especially, there had been few restrictions. Motorboats of all types were allowed anywhere on the lake and there were spots for 100 campers at the remote south end of the lake.

In 2009, the Parks Canada Warden Service was re-organized; the majority of wardens are now known as "resource management specialists." The role of the few remaining "wardens" is restricted to law enforcement, while resource managers focus on visitor safety and experience, which at Maligne Lake includes minimizing human–wildlife conflict, keeping trails clear, liaising with commercial operators such as Maligne Tours, and initiating search and rescue as required.

did the number of activities and services. In 1986, commercial whitewater rafting on the Maligne River received approval from Parks Canada. Three years later, in 1989, commercial horseback riding commenced; the most popular trip led above the treeline and into the Bald Hills. In the mid-1990s, biologists began reporting declines in the population of harlequin ducks on the Maligne River. Although the direct link was not made to increased tourism, the government banned whitewater rafting trips on the Maligne River in 1998.

Through all the advances in modern technology, there is still no phone line linking Maligne Lake to the outside world; instead there's a satellite phone and Internet link. As early as the 1940s, a lack of reliable communications to the lake led to the establishment of downtown ticket offices. They have been in a number of locations, including Tekarra Gift Shop, Jasper Camera & Gift, the Maligne Building on Connaught Drive, and in the lobby of the Jasper Park Lodge. The current Maligne Tours ticket office, on Patricia Street, opened in 2006.

Today, commercial operations at Maligne Lake—the scenic cruises, boathouse, day lodge, and shuttle bus from town—are operated by Maligne Tours. Although boat tours don't start until the ice is off the lake, Maligne Tours staff begin preparing for the season in mid-April. This company employs up to 75 people in peak season, many of which have worked out at the lake for decades. General manager Pat Crowley has worked for Maligne Tours for almost 40 years.

Although the main focus at Maligne Lake is on nature, a variety of connections to the past can be experienced. Maligne Lake Chalet, listed on the Register of the Government of Canada Heritage Buildings, has been extensively restored; canoes can be rented from Curly Phillips's boathouse, which is on the Alberta Register of Historic Places; and hikers can explore trails laid out by explorers and pioneers. Carrying on in the tradition of those linked to tourism, both Parks Canada and Maligne Tours have made great strides to ensure that the lake's history and the pristine wilderness that surrounds it are preserved for future generations of visitors.

The modern tour boats used today are a far cry from the handmade raft used by Mary Schäffer a century ago.

Bighorn sheep, Medicine Lake

Maligne Lake Road

A VISIT TO MALIGNE LAKE BEGINS WITH A WILD AND DRAMATIC DRIVE ALONG THE 45-KILOMETRE (28-MILE) MALIGNE LAKE ROAD—A WORTHY JOURNEY IN ITSELF AND A WONDERFUL INTRODUCTION TO MALIGNE LAKE.

Maligne Lake Road branches southward from the Yellowhead Highway (Highway 16) five kilometres (three miles) east of downtown Jasper. After crossing the braided Athabasca River, it quickly reaches a turn-off that leads straight to Lakes Annette and Edith, as well as the Fairmont Jasper Park Lodge. At this junction, the road curves northward and passes through open montane meadows where elk are often seen grazing.

Maligne Canyon

As the Maligne River drops into the Athabasca River valley, its gradient becomes particularly steep. It is not known exactly how the canyon formed, but one theory is that as the ice that covered the Maligne Valley during the last Ice Age melted, it dug into the valley floor and eventually wore through the bedrock to an underground passage, which created a canyon. In the estimated 14,000 years since the end of the last Ice Age, water has continued the erosion process, thereby deepening the canyon and smoothing its walls.

The most popular access point for Maligne Canyon is where Maligne Lake Road crosses the Maligne River, just over six kilometres (3.7 miles) from the Yellowhead Highway. Here you will find a large parking area, an

MALIGNE CANYON TEA ROOM

While the canyon has been popular with tourists for over 100 years, early visitors arriving by horse or carriage were usually hungry and tired after what was then a long journey from the railway. In 1914, a crude log shelter was built near the top of the canyon. It had two bedrooms for overnight guests and a living area. In 1927, Merle Brewster, wife of local outfitter Jack Brewster, opened a log tea house that overlooked the top of the canyon. The original building was replaced with a larger structure in 1963, and after a succession of owners—including Bill Ruddy, who operated boat tours at Maligne Lake for almost 30 years—the current owners took over in 1980.

interpretive kiosk, and a restaurant/gift shop complex.

From the north corner of the Maligne Canyon parking area, a trail follows the canyon downstream for 3.7 kilometres (2.3 miles). The trail crosses the canyon six times, but the most spectacular views are at the upper end of the trail, with the first two bridges being the best vantage points.

At the top of the canyon opposite the restaurant complex, you will see large potholes in the limestone riverbed. These bowl-like depressions are created when rocks and pebbles become trapped in what begins as a shallow hole; under the force of the rushing water, they carve jug-shaped hollows into the soft bedrock. Eventually, a series of these holes may lose their circular shapes completely and form a channel.

The first bridge overlooks the canyon's highest waterfall. Here, the Maligne River forces itself through a narrow opening, which creates a spectacular 22-metre (75-foot) high cascade that enters the canyon with an audible roar. Bedrock along this portion of the trail has been dated back to the late Devonian period (around 360 million years ago). At the second bridge, look for large fractures on the smooth limestone walls. While these fissures formed many millions of years ago during the mountain-building process, they have expanded as a result of water seeping through the porous limestone. In the winter, when water in the bedrock freezes, it expands and creates pressure, which forces the rock to crack further. The second bridge also marks the deepest point of the canyon—55 metres (180 feet) deep. Although the canyon is not as deep at the third bridge, here it is at its narrowest. A short way further downstream, just below the fourth bridge, is a spring fed by Medicine Lake, further up-valley.

The road to Maligne Lake was not completed and paved until 1970

HI-Maligne Canyon

HI-MALIGNE CANYON

Upstream from Maligne Canyon is HI-Maligne Canyon, the only accommodation along Maligne Lake Road. This rustic hostel, part of Hostelling International, is one of 10 wilderness hostels in the Canadian Rockies. Although it has no running water and no flush toilets, it is a great place to get back to nature while enjoying the company of like-minded travellers from around the world. Dating back to the 1940s, it comprises four small timber buildings—two dormitories, a communal kitchen/living area, and a manager's cabin.

Maligne Canyon

Sixth Bridge is accessible by road, or by a trail that begins at the top of Maligne Canyon

Although the canyon is one of the most popular natural attractions in Jasper National Park, few visitors hike the entire length of the trail. By beginning from the lower end of the canyon, at the confluence of the Maligne and Athabasca rivers, you will avoid starting your hike alongside the masses and will get to hike downhill on your return (during which you will likely be tired). To access the lower end of the canyon, follow the 1-kilometre (0.6-mile) spur off Maligne Lake Road to the sixth bridge. Crowds will be minimal for the first three kilometres (1.9 miles) to the fourth bridge, where the trail starts climbing. By the time you get to the third bridge, you will start encountering the more adventurous hikers coming down the canyon, and soon thereafter you will meet the crowds.

At the top of the canyon is Maligne Canyon Restaurant and Gift Shop, which has been a popular stop with tourists since 1927. Today, the complex offers inviting outdoor tables and a wide range of books and souvenirs. It is open from April through October.

Between Maligne Canyon and Medicine Lake

Beyond Maligne Canyon, Maligne Lake Road closely follows the Maligne River for 16 kilometres (10 miles) to Medicine Lake. The Colin Range rises dramatically to the north, and the Maligne Range lies across the river to the south. Wildlife viewing is optimal along this stretch of road; deer, elk, and black bears are commonly seen here, especially in the spring and fall.

Medicine Lake

Dramatically fluctuating water levels and no visible outlet stream make the six-kilometre-long (3.7-mile-long) Medicine Lake the most intriguing feature along Maligne Lake Road. At the lake's northwest corner, where Maligne Lake Road loops around, is a lookout with a sweeping view down the entire length of the lake. Interpretive panels tell the story of its natural history. From here, a steep path leads down to the lake itself.

Each spring, Medicine Lake fills as the snow pack from the surrounding mountains melts. By late summer, when runoff begins decreasing, the water level in the lake also begins dropping. By November, all that remains of the lake are mudflats and a few braided streams. Centuries ago, the Métis, Stoney, and Cree who travelled through the Maligne Valley could not explain why the lake disappeared. They believed that it was inhabited by dark magic, or bad medicine, hence the name. The water, however, had not disappeared; it had just begun its underground travels through an extensive network of caves. Judging from the large number of boulders clogging the valley immediately below Medicine Lake, it is apparent that the lake was at least partially formed by a massive rockslide that originated on the slopes of the Colin Range. The trapped waters of the Maligne River eventually followed passages downward into a cave system, so the water was able to escape via underground channels and resurface in the Maligne River further downstream. Today, the water follows this same course. The best way to appreciate this phenomenon is to pull off Maligne Lake Road just before reaching Medicine Lake (travelling up-valley, look for the pullout on the right) and take note of the dry riverbed at the lake's outlet.

During the 1970s, geologists performed a number of experiments to better understand how Medicine Lake's drainage system worked. Author Ben Gadd writes of one such experiment in *Handbook of the Canadian Rockies*. Red rhodamine, a dye that does not disperse in water, was introduced into the

Medicine Lake in fall, when most of the water has drained out

A black bear passes below the viewpoint at Medicine Lake

lake in order to help scientists determine how far the water travelled. The dye was found at various points in Maligne Canyon, but surprisingly, it also turned up in Lac Beauvert, which is not linked to the Maligne River by an above-ground waterway. This not only told the experts that the water was travelling a great distance but also proved that Maligne River is one of the largest underground rivers in North America. Medicine Lake continues to be a source of geological wonder, largely because the underground caves and channels through which these waters run remain unexplored.

At the southeast end of Medicine Lake is Beaver Creek Picnic Area, where picnic tables are spread throughout a forested valley. A 1.6-kilometre (1-mile) trail leads from the rear

PLUGGING MEDICINE LAKE

In the late 1920s, guides such as Curly Phillips and Fred Brewster would transport supplies down Medicine Lake by boat, but low water levels in late summer and fall made this difficult. To alleviate the problem, the lake's northern outlet was blocked with mattresses and newspapers. Although the plugs did not stop all the water from draining down to the Maligne River, apparently it did prolong navigation on the lake. Larry McGuire, the warden at Maligne Lake at that time, would collect newspapers throughout the summer to plug the outflow so that he could get his winter supplies to his cabin. Plugging of Medicine Lake continued until the early 1950s.

THE ARCH

From the pullout on the right (southwest) side of the road just beyond Medicine Lake, look up (back across the road) and you will see a natural arch on a high ridge of the Queen Elizabeth Ranges. Eroded from the limestone bedrock, the ridge is clearly visible against the blue sky on a sunny day.

The Arch

of the picnic area to Beaver Lake, a shallow body of turquoise water where waterfowl such as loons are often seen. Allow one hour for the round trip.

Continuing to Maligne Lake

From the southeast end of Maligne Lake, where Fred Brewster and Curly Phillips would unload their guests from boats and finish the journey to Maligne Lake on horseback, it is 16 kilometres (10 miles) to the end of the road. In a number of places, the road skirts close to the river, including at the Maligne River Picnic Area, where tables are spread across a grassy riverside flat. Of geological note along this stretch of road are massive boulders dotted throughout the forest. They were deposited here less than 14,000 years ago, after retreating glaciers at the end of the last Ice Age undercut layers of the Queen Elizabeth Ranges and caused a series of massive rockslides.

After cresting a low rise the road passes tiny Rose Marie Lake, and then descends to Maligne Lake. The first turn-off to the left is parking for the Maligne Tours scenic cruise, the historic boathouse, the Mary Schäffer Loop, and a lakeside picnic area. Maligne Lake Road continues beyond this point for 500 metres (0.3 miles) over the Maligne River to another parking area, a boat launch, and the trailhead for hikes to Moose Lake, Lorraine and Mona lakes, and the Bald Hills.

Just before reaching Maligne Lake, Maligne Lake Road passes Rose Marie Lake (opposite), a small body of water fed by a stream originating in the Opal Hills. The lake's water is very cold—even colder than Maligne Lake's. "Rose Marie" is an unofficial name used by locals; on official government maps, the lake is unnamed. Although no one seems to know exactly when the name came into common usage, it is probably linked to the 1954 movie, Rose Marie, which was based on a 1924 Broadway musical of the same name. The movie includes scenes filmed in the Maligne Valley (it was mostly filmed around Mammoth Lakes, California). One scene features a rock now known as Rose Marie's Rock, downstream from the lake.

Spirit Island is the scenic highlight of Maligne Lake

Enjoying Maligne Lake

GLIDE ACROSS TURQUOISE WATERS ON A SCENIC LAKE CRUISE, PADDLE TO A PRIVATE COVE AND SPREAD OUT A PICNIC LUNCH, CAST FOR FIGHTING RAINBOW TROUT, LACE UP HIKING BOOTS FOR A WILDERNESS ADVENTURE THROUGH A PRISTINE FOREST, OR SIMPLY BREATHE IN SOME INTOXICATINGLY FRESH MOUNTAIN AIR—WHO COULD ASK FOR MORE?

Maligne Lake Road terminates at the lake's north end near the Maligne Tours ticket office and large day lodge, which includes a restaurant and gift shop. Below the main parking area is Curly Phillips's historic boathouse, where you can rent canoes and kayaks. Walk along the shoreline from the boathouse and you will find picnic tables scattered through the open lakeside meadow. Maligne Lake Road continues a short distance beyond the Maligne Tours complex and over the Maligne River to a large parking area, a boat launch, and a forest with picnic tables. This is also the starting point for trails to Moose Lake, Lorraine and Mona lakes, and the Bald Hills.

Lake Cruise

While the view of Maligne Lake from the end of the road is stunning, the views are even better further down the lake, where glacial runoff turns the water an enchanting turquoise colour and mountain peaks seemingly jostle each other for lakeside superiority. Taking a boat tour is an absolute must.

In 1908, Mary Schäffer and her guides fashioned a raft from trees and paddled onto Maligne Lake. Today, visitors can enjoy the same lake-and-mountain panorama enjoyed by Schäffer over a century ago from the comfort of a covered tour boat on a 90-minute scenic cruise to Spirit Island. The only company licensed to operate on the lake is Maligne Tours, which has been taking visitors out on the lake for over 80 years.

The boat tour to Spirit Island is hosted by a tour guide who is well versed on the natural and human history of the lake, and the commentary begins as the boat departs the dock at what is locally known as Home Bay. Passengers learn about the ancient rockslides that spread across the valley, the geology of prominent peaks, and the local wildlife. As the boat continues towards Spirit Island, the origins of the surrounding mountains are explained; the guide describes their composition and points out features such as the Opal Hills and fault lines. As the boat motors southward, a number of glaciers come into view, and the geology of these frozen rivers of ice clinging to the mountains is explained.

When entering Samson Narrows (also called The Narrows), it becomes apparent that sediment runoff from the surrounding mountains has accumulated in the lake, as the lake's width is just 100 metres (330 feet) here. Beyond Samson Narrows, the tour boats round a corner and the famous Spirit Island comes into view. Here, the captain will turn

TOUR BOATS

Most of the eight boats that Maligne Tours uses were built by Canoe Cove Manufacturing, based on Vancouver Island, British Columbia. The boats seat up to 56 passengers, and the large windows, open back deck, and covered cabins make them perfect for touring the lake in all weather.

The oldest boat in the fleet is *Mary Schäffer*. It was built in 1968 and seats 38 passengers. Seating just 10 passengers, the smallest boat is *Curly*, named for Donald "Curly" Phillips.

Samson Beaver is named for the Stoney friend of Mary Schäffer who drew the 1911 map of Maligne Lake. Also honouring this era is *Chaba III*, named for the rafts used by Mary Schäffer during her 1908 and 1911 visits to Maligne Lake. *Bill Ruddy* is named in honour of a former owner of Maligne Tours, while *John Albert* is named for

The Maligne Tours dock

John Albert (Jack) Hargreaves, Ruddy's father-in-law. *Lisa L* is named for the daughter of another Maligne Tours owner, Gerry Levasseur, who bought the business from Ruddy.

As any sailor knows, it is bad luck to change a boat's name, so *Talana*, which previously operated on Shuswap Lake in British Columbia, has a name with no link to Maligne Lake.

off the boat's motor and allow passengers to step out onto the boat's deck and soak up the 360-degree lake-and-mountain panorama. After the captain steers the boat ashore to a dock beside Spirit Island, plenty of time is allotted to walk the short trail to the ideal vantage—a postcard-perfect composition of Spirit Island surrounded by turquoise water and Mount Charlton rising dramatically in the background.

The lookout over Spirit Island, a small isle of trees linked to the mainland by a low, rocky isthmus, provides one of the most famous vistas in the Canadian Rockies and is surely one of the most recognized mountain scenes in all of Canada. In the early 1920s, James B. Harkin, Dominion Parks Branch commissioner, contracted Calgary photographer William J. Oliver to take photographs of the Canadian Rockies as part of a publicity campaign to entice tourists to the mountain parks. The most recognizable of Oliver's photographs is a sepia-toned scene featuring Spirit Island, a birch canoe, and a tepee. This highly stylized image created a romantic visual that left viewers with an impression of Maligne Lake that was remote, wild, and connected to Aboriginal mysticism. Renowned Banff photographer Byron Harmon visited the island in 1924 and staged a photo shoot that also used a tepee. In the 1940s and 50s, local photographer Harry Rowed became known as much for his large-format images of the park as his popular postcards that were sold at his Jasper studio. Rowed often called the island "F11" for the camera setting that produced the best photographs.

It was not until the late 1960s that the name Spirit Island came into widespread use. Although the name is now inextricably linked to the beauty of Maligne Lake and Jasper National Park, its origin is not known. One story involves the nephew of Suzette Swift, who homesteaded in the Athabasca River Valley in the 1890s. It is said that the young boy became sick and died on a hunting trip to the lake and is buried on what the family began calling "Spirit Island."

After leaving Spirit Island, the tour boat returns to Home Bay. The official commentary will have been completed at this point, and so this part of the tour is a great opportunity to sit back, relax, and soak up the scenery.

The scenic cruise runs multiple times daily between early June and early October, weather permitting. To avoid the crowds and for the best chance of enjoying calm water, plan to join an early morning or late afternoon cruise. Make reservations in advance either at the company's downtown ticket office or the office out at the lake, or book online at www.malignelake.com.

MALIGNE LAKE IN NEW YORK

In 1950, the Kodak company launched a Colorama display at New York's Grand Central Terminal. For 40 years, a different image would be displayed every few weeks. Coined "the world's largest photograph," Coloramas were photographs that were enlarged and transferred to transparencies measuring 5.5 metres (18 feet) high by 18 metres (60 feet) wide. These oversized colour transparencies were backlit; the technology used was similar to that behind colour slides but on a larger scale. The Colorama was not only an advertisement for Kodak's technological advances but was also a celebration of photography itself; many of the Coloramas depicted people taking photographs.

For eight weeks over the summer of 1960, all of New York was able to experience the beauty of Maligne Lake when the featured Colorama was "Jasper National Park," which featured Spirit Island. The Maligne Lake image was taken by Pete Gales, who came to prominence as a photographer during World War II while serving with the U.S. Navy.

Rent canoes and kayaks from the boathouse

Canoeing and Kayaking

Both canoeing and kayaking are fantastic ways to enjoy the wilderness at a leisurely pace. Some paddlers bring their own craft, but most rent from the boathouse, on the lakeshore in front of the day lodge. For those with little or no paddling experience, canoes are easier to get in and out of and have more room to store gear. The advantage of renting a kayak is the extra stability and speed. Within easy paddling distance of the boathouse are a number of picturesque bays—the perfect place to enjoy a picnic lunch. Before heading out onto the lake, be sure to check weather forecasts and try to stay as close to the shoreline as possible.

Those not afraid to rough it can take advantage of two lakeside campgrounds that can only be reached by canoe or kayak. Located at Fisherman's Bay (just north of

Spirit Island), and at the mouth of Coronet Creek (at the remote south end of the lake), they are primitive facilities that require campers to be totally self-sufficient. For information and reservations, contact Parks Canada (www.parkscanada.gc.ca) or visit the downtown Jasper Visitor Centre.

Canoeing on Maligne Lake

Gift Shop

Muffins are baked in-house daily

Lunch at the day lodge

Maligne Tours ticket office

Fishing

Since Curly Phillips built his boathouse in 1929, fishing has been one of the most popular pastimes at Maligne Lake. Although no species are native to the lake, brook trout (also called speckled trout or "brookies") were introduced to Maligne Lake as sport fish in 1928, and the government stocking program continued through to the early 1970s. This colourful fish is easily identified by its dark green back with pale-coloured splotches and by its sides, which have a purple-sheen. In Maligne Lake, they average 0.7 to one kilograms (1.5 to 2.2 pounds), but the record for Maligne Lake stands at 5.8 kilograms (12 pounds 13 ounces). No one knows exactly how rainbow trout found their way to Maligne Lake, but it is assumed that they were introduced sometime before the 1960s. The rainbow trout in Maligne Lake average 1.4 to 2.3 kilograms (three to five pounds), although bigger fish are often reported, including the Alberta record, which weighed in at 9.3 kilograms (20 pounds four ounces).

Stocking ended decades ago, but Maligne Lake now has self-sustaining populations of both species. Brook trout are a schooling fish that congregate around creek mouths or structures such as docks, while rainbow trout are solitary fish that are more evenly distributed throughout the lake. The predictable habitat of brook trout makes them popular with some anglers, while the unpredictability and fighting spirit of rainbow trout makes them the preferred species for anglers looking for a challenge. Of the many fishing techniques used at Maligne Lake, trolling a sinking fly line with a minnow pattern or dry casting chironomids (midges) are most popular with locals. Although most of the focus for anglers is on the better-known Maligne Lake, Medicine Lake has a healthy population

FISH STOCKING

Although the government first began looking into stocking lakes in the Canadian Rockies specifically for the purpose of sport fishing soon after the creation of Banff National Park, in 1885, it was not until 1925 that stocking was considered in Jasper, where glacier-fed lakes like Maligne did not support natural populations of fish. Stocking began in the late 1920s with the release of brown trout fry in small lakes close to the Jasper townsite, including Lakes Edith and Annette. The park's first hatchery was an old cabin beside Cabin Creek, but the operation had been relocated to the basement of the Park Administration Building (now the Park Visitor Centre) by 1930. Maligne Lake was first stocked in 1928, when 190,000 brook trout fry were transported by packhorse up the Maligne Valley. Similar numbers were released over ensuing years, and by 1932, trout measuring up to 46 centimetres (18 inches) were being reported in Maligne Lake.

As the park's stocking program become too large for the basement of the Administration Building, a purpose-built hatchery was opened in 1942 on the Maligne River, just upstream from its confluence with the Athabasca River. Fingerlings hatched at this facility were released into Medicine and Maligne Lakes, as well as lakes throughout western Canada's national parks. By this time, fishing was a major draw in Jasper National Park, and Maligne Lake was the focus of anglers from around the world. The decision to close the hatchery in 1973 was met with resistance from many locals, including the Jasper Chamber of Commerce, but the end of the stocking program did not mark the end of fishing in the park, which is still a popular pastime for both locals and visitors.

of rainbow trout, where only fly-fishing is permitted).

One of the best ways to ensure a successful fishing trip is to hire a guide. A number of companies offer guided fishing, including On-Line Sport and Tackle and Maligne Tours; both offer the option of half- or full-day trips. Usually, boat rental, tackle, and lunch are included. For those wanting to fishing without a guide, boat and tackle rentals are available at the boathouse as well as at sports stores in the town of Jasper. All anglers fishing at Maligne Lake require a Parks Canada fishing permit (the Alberta sportfishing licence is not recognized within the national park). Maligne Lake is open for fishing from mid-May to the end of September, while Medicine Lake is open through to the end of October.

Preparing for a fishing trip

Hiking

While most visitors to the area focus on Maligne Lake itself and its boat tours, there are a number of memorable hiking trails starting from the north end of the lake. Easy trails lead along both sides of the lake, and some lead to smaller lakes in the surrounding forest. More strenuous outings involve climbing surrounding mountain slopes above the treeline for sweeping views.

Although wildlife is present throughout the Maligne Valley, you should be especially aware when hiking. The Jasper Visitor Centre, in downtown Jasper, issues regular trail reports, or check for bulletins posted at trailhead kiosks. Special caution should be taken on the Opal Hills Trail, where grizzly bears roam throughout late spring and summer.

MARY SCHÄFFER LOOP
Also known as the Lake Trail, this 3.2-kilometre (two-mile) loop can easily be completed in one hour and has minimal

Looking across to Mts. Charlton and Unwin from the Mary Schäffer Viewpoint

Lakeshore Trail panorama

elevation gain. This pleasant walk begins at the historic boathouse. A paved path runs through an open area of lakeside picnic tables at Picnic Point to Schäffer Viewpoint, named for the explorer who is associated with putting Maligne Lake on the map. Across the lake from the viewpoint is the Maligne Range, and, to the southwest, the distinctive twin peaks of Mount Unwin and Mount Charlton. After dragging yourself away from the spectacular panorama, continue along a shallow bay before following the trail into a coniferous forest of lodgepole pine and spruce and then looping back to the main parking lot.

LAKESHORE TRAIL

Across the lake, an unofficial trail that starts from the public boat launch leads along the south shoreline for just over 1 kilometre (0.6 miles). Although one will not have the same view down Maligne Lake enjoyed along the Mary Schäffer Loop, this trail is quieter and does have sweeping views across the lake to the Opal Hills. It also passes stretches of pebbly beach. From the boat launch, follow the Moose Lake trail past the Parks Canada dock and keep left when the main trail jogs away from the lake into the forest. Here, you can enjoy a walk through a typical subalpine forest of lodgepole pine and spruce. Look around and you will see a forest floor covered in fallen trees engulfed in mosses, flowers such as arnica, and even mushrooms. The trail ends at south-facing pebbly beach—the perfect place to contemplate the surrounding mountainscape. Allow around 15 or 20 minutes to reach the end of the trail.

MOOSE LAKE

The under three-kilometre (1.9 mile) loop trail that passes by Moose Lake can be completed in one hour and is one of the most enjoyable, easy hikes in the vicinity of Maligne Lake. Park in the large parking area at the very end of Maligne Lake Road and then walk uphill across the road to the trailhead kiosk at a locked gate. From here, follow the wide Opal Hills trail for 300 metres (0.2 miles) and then turn left onto a narrow pathway that crosses a stream and disappears into the forest. One kilometre (0.6 miles) along this trail, a rough track branches left and leads to Moose Lake—a quiet body of water where moose are sometimes seen just after dawn. To return to the parking lot, continue along the trail as it descends to the shore of Maligne Lake. Here, you have the option to continue left to the parking lot or extend your walk by heading right along the Lakeshore Trail.

LORRAINE AND MONA LAKES

These forest-encircled lakes take longer to reach than Moose Lake but are both delightful destinations that can be combined into a 5.6-kilometre (3.5-mile), two-hour roundtrip (or longer if you bring a picnic lunch). The trailhead is 100 metres north (to the right) of the trailhead for Moose Lake and the Bald Hills, across the road from the parking lot at the very end of Maligne Lake Road. The well-formed trail rises and falls through a subalpine

Lorraine Lake

Moose Lake

Well-formed hiking trails radiate from Maligne Lake

forest of mostly lodgepole pine. The uneven topography was created by a rockslide less than 14,000 years ago; along the first section of trail is a steep-sided hollow created by fallen rock. After two kilometres (1.3 miles) of easy hiking, a signed trail leads left at a small pond to Lorraine Lake, which is named for the daughter of Larry and Hilda Magistad, managers for Curly Phillips's widow in the 1940s.

The turnoff to Mona Lake is 300 metres (0.2 miles) further along the main trail. It takes less than five minutes to reach both lakes from the main trail. Mona Lake is the larger of the two and offers views north down the Maligne Valley. It also has a more picturesque rocky shoreline.

BALD HILLS

The all uphill journey to the Bald Hills is a moderately strenuous 5.2-kilometre (3.2 mile) hike that gains around 500 metres (1,640 feet) of elevation, but the rewards are ample—a sweeping panorama of Maligne Lake and distant mountains, including the twin peaks of Mount Unwin and Mount Charlton to the south and, across the lake, the Queen Elizabeth Ranges. The trail follows an old fire road the entire way to the official end of the trail and passes through an area of lodgepole pine before entering the upper subalpine zone of stunted alpine fir and Engelmann spruce. The trail officially ends at the site of a fire lookout, which has been removed. Beyond the lookout site are seemingly endless alpine meadows. You can easily spend an hour or more exploring the meadows, viewing the antics of marmots and pikas, or identifying the many colourful species of wildflowers. For the energetic, the option is available to continue the climb by ascending one of the rocky ridges the hills are named for. The trailhead is the same as Moose Lake. Follow Maligne Lake Road across the Maligne River to the parking lot and walk back across the road to the locked gate at the base of the fire road.

Allow two and a half to three hours for the roundtrip to the fire lookout site, plus at least an hour or two for exploring the meadows.

OPAL HILLS

Opposite the Bald Hills, on the east side of Maligne Lake, lie the iron-coloured Opal Hills (to the left as you gaze down the lake from the day lodge). An 8.2-kilometre (5.1-mile) trail loops over their lower slopes, which are not the true Opal Hills but high ridges of boulders created by an ancient rockslide. The roundtrip distance is shorter than the trail that leads up to the Bald Hills and back down, but as this trail is steeper, you should allow the same amount of time for both— approximately two and a half to three hours. Beginning from the far corner of the upper parking area beside the day lodge, the trail passes through a subalpine forest dotted with boulders from an ancient rockslide. After 1.6 kilometres (1.0 miles) of steady climbing, the

Pikas are common among the boulders of the Opal Hills

trail forks. This is the start of a 4.8-kilometre (three-mile) loop. The trail to the left gains elevation more slowly than the one to the right, which makes a steep, quick climb above the treeline. Views from the trail summit are not as expansive as from the Bald Hills, but the view is stunning nonetheless.

Looking down to Maligne Lake from the Bald Hills

Photo Credits

All contemporary photos © 2011 by Andrew Hempstead, except where noted.

Summerthought Publishing would like to thank the following for permission to reproduce their archival images:

Glenbow Archives: p. 42 (na-568-1)

Jasper Yellowhead Museum and Archives: p. 3 (2009.68.01.45), p. 48 (CAJ vol. 4, 1912, p.94), p. 52 (top; PA38-7), p. 52 (bottom; PA38-8), p. 53 (2009.68.01.31), p. 56 (top; 994.45.118a), p. 56 (bottom; 994.45.119a), page 57 (PA7-98), p. 58 (990.63.15), p. 59 (990.28.184.01), p. 60 (994.45.26a.1), p. 61 (994.45.112.3), p. 62 (001.33.244), p. 63 (001.33.202), p. 64 (997.07.180.17), p. 66 (top; 994.45.121a), p. 67 (994.45.74), p. 68 (001.33.10), p. 72 (000.34.249), p. 73 (top; PA69-13), back cover (Maligne Tours back cover, top left)National Gallery of Canada: p. 54

Whyte Museum of the Canadian Rockies: p. 40-41 (na71-2294), p. 43 (v527-pd1-90207/2; Mary Schäffer), p. 44 (top; v527-ng-124; Mary Schäffer), p. 44 (bottom; v527-ps1-53; Mary Schäffer), p. 45 (v527-pd1-1; Mary Schäffer), p. 46 (v527-ps1-61; Mary Schäffer), p. 47 (v527-ps1-131; Mary Schäffer), p. 49 (top; v527-pd1-a20443; Mary Schäffer), p. 49 (bottom; v488-blk27-23-24-25; Parks Canada), p. 50 (v90-pc-1-na66-1962), p. 51 (v263-na-1136; Byron Harmon), p. 65 (v227-4136; Bill Gibbons), p. 66 (bottom; v92-pd2-1; Rainbow Tours), back cover (Maligne Tours back cover, top right; v527-ps1-136; Mary Schäffer)

About the Author

As a Jasper resident, Meghan Power has explored the Maligne Valley from one end to the other—she has joined tourists from around the world on the scenic lake cruise, hiked the many trails surrounding the lake, cross-country skied through the valley, and travelled from one end of Maligne Canyon to the other, as well as enjoyed simple pleasures, such as a summer picnic along the lakeshore. Through all these experiences and more, she has gained a profound appreciation for what many regard as one of the most beautiful destinations in Canada. When she's not out exploring the national park she calls home, Meghan can be found working as the archivist at the Jasper Yellowhead Museum & Archives.

Acknowledgments

Thanks to the following people for helping during the research of this book: Joy Phillips, for sharing her memories of her parents, Curly and Grace; former Jasper National Park wardens Mac Elder and Toni Klettl for their recollections of living at the lake; the insights of Mike Wesbrook, the present-day Resource Management and Public Safety Specialist for the Maligne Lake District; Mike Dillion, Cultural Resource specialist for Jasper National Park; Mickey Bleskie for his stories of Fred Brewster and his father, Nick; Tom Peterson, for his thoughts on working at Brewster's camp; Ben Gadd, for generously sharing his vast knowledge of the geology of the Maligne Valley; Gordon Ruddy, for sharing his family memories of growing up at Maligne Lake; Karen Byers, for sharing her stories of summer employment with Maligne Tours; and Pat Crowley, general manager of Maligne Tours, who helped through all phases of research and production. I would also like to thank the Jasper Yellowhead Historical Society Board for their unwavering dedication to the preservation of Jasper National Park's history. Finally, I would like to thank Summerthought Publishing for giving me the opportunity to be a part this special project.